CW00546913

HowExpert Guide to Fantasy Football

101 Tips to Learn How to Play, Strategize, and Win at Fantasy Football

HowExpert with Bobby Duke

Copyright HowExpert™
www.HowExpert.com

For more tips related to this topic, visit HowExpert.com/fantasyfootball.

Recommended Resources

- HowExpert.com – Quick 'How To' Guides on All Topics from A to Z by Everyday Experts.
- HowExpert.com/free – Free HowExpert Email Newsletter.
- HowExpert.com/books – HowExpert Books
- HowExpert.com/courses – HowExpert Courses
- HowExpert.com/clothing – HowExpert Clothing
- HowExpert.com/membership – HowExpert Membership Site
- HowExpert.com/affiliates – HowExpert Affiliate Program
- HowExpert.com/jobs – HowExpert Jobs
- HowExpert.com/writers – Write About Your #1 Passion/Knowledge/Expertise & Become a HowExpert Author.
- HowExpert.com/resources – Additional HowExpert Recommended Resources
- YouTube.com/HowExpert – Subscribe to HowExpert YouTube.
- Instagram.com/HowExpert – Follow HowExpert on Instagram.
- Facebook.com/HowExpert – Follow HowExpert on Facebook.

Publisher's Foreword

Dear HowExpert Reader,

HowExpert publishes quick 'how to' guides on all topics from A to Z by everyday experts.

At HowExpert, our mission is to discover, empower, and maximize everyday people's talents to ultimately make a positive impact in the world for all topics from A to Z...one everyday expert at a time!

All of our HowExpert guides are written by everyday people just like you and me, who have a passion, knowledge, and expertise for a specific topic.

We take great pride in selecting everyday experts who have a passion, real-life experience in a topic, and excellent writing skills to teach you about the topic you are also passionate about and eager to learn.

We hope you get a lot of value from our HowExpert guides, and it can make a positive impact on your life in some way. All of our readers, including you, help us continue living our mission of positively impacting the world for all spheres of influences from A to Z.

If you enjoyed one of our HowExpert guides, then please take a moment to send us your feedback from wherever you got this book.

Thank you, and we wish you all the best in all aspects of life.

Sincerely,

BJ Min
Founder & Publisher of HowExpert
HowExpert.com

PS...If you are also interested in becoming a HowExpert author, then please visit our website at **HowExpert.com/writers**. Thank you & again, all the best!

COPYRIGHT, LEGAL NOTICE AND DISCLAIMER:

COPYRIGHT © BY HOWEXPERT™ (OWNED BY HOT METHODS). ALL RIGHTS RESERVED WORLDWIDE. NO PART OF THIS PUBLICATION MAY BE REPRODUCED IN ANY FORM OR BY ANY MEANS, INCLUDING SCANNING, PHOTOCOPYING, OR OTHERWISE WITHOUT PRIOR WRITTEN PERMISSION OF THE COPYRIGHT HOLDER.

DISCLAIMER AND TERMS OF USE: PLEASE NOTE THAT MUCH OF THIS PUBLICATION IS BASED ON PERSONAL EXPERIENCE AND ANECDOTAL EVIDENCE. ALTHOUGH THE AUTHOR AND PUBLISHER HAVE MADE EVERY REASONABLE ATTEMPT TO ACHIEVE COMPLETE ACCURACY OF THE CONTENT IN THIS GUIDE, THEY ASSUME NO RESPONSIBILITY FOR ERRORS OR OMISSIONS. ALSO, YOU SHOULD USE THIS INFORMATION AS YOU SEE FIT, AND AT YOUR OWN RISK. YOUR PARTICULAR SITUATION MAY NOT BE EXACTLY SUITED TO THE EXAMPLES ILLUSTRATED HERE; IN FACT, IT'S LIKELY THAT THEY WON'T BE THE SAME, AND YOU SHOULD ADJUST YOUR USE OF THE INFORMATION AND RECOMMENDATIONS ACCORDINGLY.

THE AUTHOR AND PUBLISHER DO NOT WARRANT THE PERFORMANCE, EFFECTIVENESS OR APPLICABILITY OF ANY SITES LISTED OR LINKED TO IN THIS BOOK. ALL LINKS ARE FOR INFORMATION PURPOSES ONLY AND ARE NOT WARRANTED FOR CONTENT, ACCURACY OR ANY OTHER IMPLIED OR EXPLICIT PURPOSE.

ANY TRADEMARKS, SERVICE MARKS, PRODUCT NAMES OR NAMED FEATURES ARE ASSUMED TO BE THE PROPERTY OF THEIR RESPECTIVE OWNERS, AND ARE USED ONLY FOR REFERENCE. THERE IS NO IMPLIED ENDORSEMENT IF WE USE ONE OF THESE TERMS.

NO PART OF THIS BOOK MAY BE REPRODUCED, STORED IN A RETRIEVAL SYSTEM, OR TRANSMITTED BY ANY OTHER MEANS: ELECTRONIC, MECHANICAL, PHOTOCOPYING, RECORDING, OR OTHERWISE, WITHOUT THE PRIOR WRITTEN PERMISSION OF THE AUTHOR.

ANY VIOLATION BY STEALING THIS BOOK OR DOWNLOADING OR SHARING IT ILLEGALLY WILL BE PROSECUTED BY LAWYERS TO THE FULLEST EXTENT. THIS PUBLICATION IS PROTECTED UNDER THE US COPYRIGHT ACT OF 1976 AND ALL OTHER APPLICABLE INTERNATIONAL, FEDERAL, STATE AND LOCAL LAWS AND ALL RIGHTS ARE RESERVED, INCLUDING RESALE RIGHTS: YOU ARE NOT ALLOWED TO GIVE OR SELL THIS GUIDE TO ANYONE ELSE.

THIS PUBLICATION IS DESIGNED TO PROVIDE ACCURATE AND AUTHORITATIVE INFORMATION WITH REGARD TO THE SUBJECT MATTER COVERED. IT IS SOLD WITH THE UNDERSTANDING THAT THE AUTHORS AND PUBLISHERS ARE NOT ENGAGED IN RENDERING LEGAL, FINANCIAL, OR OTHER PROFESSIONAL ADVICE. LAWS AND PRACTICES OFTEN VARY FROM STATE TO STATE AND IF LEGAL OR OTHER EXPERT ASSISTANCE IS REQUIRED, THE SERVICES OF A PROFESSIONAL SHOULD BE SOUGHT. THE AUTHORS AND PUBLISHER SPECIFICALLY DISCLAIM ANY LIABILITY THAT IS INCURRED FROM THE USE OR APPLICATION OF THE CONTENTS OF THIS BOOK.

COPYRIGHT BY HOWEXPERT™ (OWNED BY HOT METHODS)
ALL RIGHTS RESERVED WORLDWIDE.

Table of Contents

Introduction: What's the Big Deal with Fantasy Football Anyway?

Hi there. It's probably safe to say you have at least *some* interest in this 'pretend' sport that people always seem to be talking about. I mean, you opened up to the first page of this book, right? Perhaps you chose to glance at it because your friends needed one more person to fill up their fantasy football league, and you were the one who got suckered into it. Maybe they mentioned to you that you just select some players and see how they perform on the field each week, and you figured, *how hard can that be?*

Possibly you enjoy kicking back and watching the games on Sunday afternoons, and you thought to yourself, *let's see if this can add to my excitement for the NFL* (National Football League, for you beginners out there). People are always talking about how fantasy football can add another dimension of fun for fans, so why not give it a try?

A more unconventional route is you saw the word 'fantasy' and your mind jumped to Dungeons and Dragons mistakenly only to realize this has nothing to do with role-playing games. Instead, it involves scoring touchdowns while using statistics and an app on your phone - which left you thoroughly confused.

I mean, what's the big deal with this whole 'imaginary' sports game anyway? How are people so obsessed with something that requires them to *literally* just choose people projected to 'do good stuff' during a football game and then see if that stuff really happens? Is it strictly so you can earn bragging rights over your peers in a little friendly competition? Can you only play this game if you spend your Sundays watching football games? Do you have to care about math? And how the heck do you play - even more, succeed - at this incredibly speculative game?

If any of these sum up your thoughts when coming across this book, well, my friend, you have come to the right place. Not only will the next few chapters prepare you with all you need to participate in the highly-coveted world of fantasy football, but they will provide you with the tools needed to better your opponents week in and week out. The information on these pages will help your friends realize who the master of football knowledge truly is (or has become) in your group.

This book will cover beginner to advanced topics through 101 key points sprinkled throughout the various chapters to help novice players learn the ropes and succeed. We will discuss the game's different rules and point systems to ensure you know what you're getting yourself into. We'll also navigate various strategies to draft the perfect team that can set the tone for the entire season with your new franchise.

Most importantly, we will take a deep dive into how to effectively manage your squad throughout the season, as your new role as the team leader can make or break your year. And lastly, we'll even break down the array of different fantasy football leagues you can join. That's right. Once you think you've got your league all figured out, the wonderful fantasy gods of the professional football world offer us an array of alternative ways to enjoy your newfound addiction.

Maybe this is right up your alley, and you're licking your chomps at the idea to use your knowledge and love for the game of football to best your friends at a new competitive endeavor. Or, maybe this all sounds overwhelming and outside of your wheelhouse like it will be way too much work. After reading through the chapters in this book, you will no longer be mindlessly scrolling down your newsfeed while waiting for your morning coffee to finish brewing. Instead, you'll be engrossed over which wide receiver you should add to your fantasy team before your next game because your top-scoring one pulled his hamstring.

Are you ready to jump in? You will become equipped with the knowledge and excitement needed to enjoy and succeed at one of the world's most popular pastimes. And you will soon understand the obsession that is buzzing around fantasy football. It will be hard to remember what the autumn months were like without this beautiful game in your life after absorbing all of the details this book has to offer. Whether you are a football fan or not, your newly-acclaimed interest and level of comprehension will have you debating with some of the sport's most established fans about your entertaining new hobby.

Chapter 1: The Ins and Outs

Tip 1: Get excited to play the most fun game on Earth.

Fantasy football is based on what players can do on the real-life football field each week with their respective teams. If a player gains yards, scores touchdowns, or completes another statistical feat in the *real* NFL game, this can translate to points for your team if you have that player on your *fantasy* roster. It brings the fun and excitement of the game of football to an entirely different level that will most likely make you wish you had started playing sooner.

This chapter will discuss the ins and outs of which positions you will need on your fantasy team, along with the rules and scoring systems surrounding your league and its players. This introduction to the different league settings will start to give you a feel for the logistics behind winning games, taking you one step closer to a chance at that coveted first place finish we all desire.

The Positions

Before we jump into the various rules and scoring systems of your new strategic sports endeavor, it is essential to understand the positions of the players you will be focusing on when building your team. What roles do you need to create a fantasy team? In short - it depends. Now, this answer will be given surrounding multiple *items* throughout this book, but I'll elaborate each time so you will have more of an idea of why this is (and so you don't just think I'm just making things up as I go along).

Tip 2: Know what positions you have to account for in your league.

This generic 'it depends' answer that you'll hear as we dig into the weeds of these fantasy football topics is because not all leagues are the same. To begin, though, we'll look at some **standard** league settings. If there are no special positional changes by your commissioner (yes, there is someone in charge of your league who will treat this role as if they are the CEO of a world-renowned company), this is what your league positions and quantities will look like:

Starting Lineup:

Quarterback (QB) - 1

Running Back (RB) - 2

Wide Receiver (WR) - 2

Tight End (TE) - 1

Flex Position (FLEX) - 1

Team Defense/Special Teams (DEF or DST) - 1

Kicker (K) - 1

There are also several bench players (BEN), usually between five and eight, that help build your team's depth. Your bench can contain a collection of players at multiple positions, not limited to any particular ones. There can potentially be injured reserve (IR) spots as well, which are spots to stash players who are hurt that don't count towards your total roster count. When players in your IR slots regain full health, you can bring them back to your active roster pending you release a different player. We'll dive into all kinds of situations involving adding and removing players as we move through the chapters of this book.

The flex position is a unique one on the roster as it allows 'flexibility' (get it?) in choosing from a few different types of players to plug in this slot. You can select an additional running back, wide receiver, or tight end for this roster spot.

With most of these positions being offensive players (people who have the opportunity to gain yards and score points when their team has possession of the ball on the gridiron), the team defense/special teams and kickers are the lone exceptions. We'll discuss how their points are tallied in standard leagues in the next section.

Tip 3: Have a good balance of positions on your bench.

There may be five amazing quarterbacks available in your league, but is it wise to have all of them when only one will get to play for your team at a time? When you select players for your fantasy roster, you will have the option to choose several bench players on your squad as well. These can become a *crucial* part of your strategy week after week, as you will encounter starters on your team who get hurt, have bye weeks (weeks where a player's NFL team has a week off so they won't play), or have a difficult matchup you feel will hinder their performance. You have the ability to have *any* player at *any* position on your bench as an alternative option for your starting team, so it's important to have adequate depth at several places.

A major point to note here, though, is that the points your players accumulate while they are on your bench are not counted towards your weekly total. It is part of the strategy of picking the correct players for your starting lineup versus who to keep on your bench for later weeks.

Tip 4: Focus on multiple options for your flex position players.

Since the flex position is such a versatile one, it is vital to take advantage of having several options for that slot available on your bench. While it can't hurt to have a backup quarterback, having additional running backs and wide receivers (in particular) are extremely valuable as you need at *least* two of each in your starting roster regularly. Possibly a third if you decide to put one in your FLEX. These players are the most unique because of the sheer quantity required for your lineup. One of the most important aspects of succeeding at fantasy football is giving yourself options week in and week out. The FLEX slot opens the door for you to have a strategic advantage with the choices you make while, at the same time, increasing the depth of some of your most vital positions.

If you're thoroughly overwhelmed already, don't worry. In Chapters 2 and 3, we'll explore in *much* more detail how to go about selecting these different positions and when is the best time to do so.

Now that you know which positions you will need to fill your lineup, what can they do for your team? Let's check out some of the standard rules in fantasy football to get you on track to becoming victorious.

The Rules

Being a part of a fantasy league may get you to glance at the television during Sunday football games for more than just your favorite adult beverage commercial. Funny story; when I first met my wife, she had absolutely *zero* interest in football (quite the opposite of me). So, when I wanted to plop down on the couch in front of the TV for 10 hours every Sunday during fall, you can imagine how some conflict ensued. However, because many of our friends were in my fantasy league when one dropped out, I suggested my wife join. I cleverly coerced her by saying *don't you want to be a part of something all of our friends are interested in every weekend?* Well, my logic lasted - for a little while. It backfired when she beat me in the championship in her first year of playing - true story. Let's just say I took partial credit for her accolade since I generously encouraged her to join (although the feeling was not reciprocated).

The point behind this unfortunate anecdote (or hilarious one if you ask my wife) is that no matter your interest level, there are plenty of opportunities to succeed in your newfound interest with the right understanding of the rules.

Overall, it's pretty simple. ***The fantasy team with the most points at the end of the week wins.*** But like any other game, there is more to it than that.

While there are a good number of rules involved with fantasy football scoring, they streamline amongst typical positional roles and relate closely and often to the real-life game. For example, every time a player gets a touchdown (except for the quarterback), that player receives six points for your fantasy squad - the same number of points a team would get in an actual football game for the same accomplishment.

Before we get too deep into the scoring, though, let's go over some of the basics for the setup of your league.

Tip 5: Read over your league's settings before the start of the season, which goes over all of the rules and the entire scoring system.

Every league has a league settings page which is overlooked by many, as it seems like a plethora of bureaucratic junk. Why read the fine print when you can just pick good players and do well (ideally)? Knowing the specifics behind how your league scores points and what rules it follows can give you a tremendous advantage in the race for first place.

Tip 6: If you have the option, compare different fantasy football platforms to determine your preference.

Fantasy football is played on an online website/smartphone application. There are also different 'standard' rules across these various platforms. While every one of them allows customization, other people have specific preferences based on the variety of settings used when playing in each of these applications. Ease of use is a huge part of any technology-user's experience, and fantasy football sites are no different. Yahoo, ESPN, and NFL Fantasy are the most common apps and websites used to play fantasy football, although there are many lesser-known products available to use as well.

Each platform has countless experts that project how players will perform each week and provide rankings and statistics based on their teams' matchups. It can be very useful information to explore on each application as well, to get a feel for their unique qualities. I will tell you that newcomers tend to get super attached to these projections, though; don't let them set your decisions in stone. Realize, when a player is projected to reach 18.32 fantasy points on one platform and 14.61 on another, there is a *minimal* chance either of them will be exactly right.

Here's something to think about with point predictions as well: let's say you didn't know a specific cornerback plays exceptionally well against wide receivers on a defense that is, overall, ranked pretty poorly. In this scenario, projections will anticipate a wide receiver to perform *well* because they are playing a generally weak passing defense. But if there is a specific 'bright spot' at the cornerback position (like in this example), this could be overlooked from a simple projection.

There are also many external sites that give advice for players every week of the NFL season. So, like anything else you try to find accuracy in, research various legitimate sources to help you fully grasp what you are looking for. Focus more on finding different analysts and resources that explain the game that caters to your gaps in knowledge and ones that are as unbiased as possible. Choosing a platform that fit's your overall needs the best is the priority.

Tip 7: Have some sort of wager for the season.
It's totally worth it.

By no means am I encouraging people to gamble if
they find no interest in doing so. Fantasy sports can
walk a fine line between gambling and friendly wagers
at times, but I am referring to the latter with this
statement. For years, as a broke college student and a
young professional after that, I just couldn't believe I
got to play this fantastic game with all of my friends,
absolutely free. All of the major platforms allow you
to play in any standard fantasy football league without
spending a dime, but I'm here to tell you, it makes it
100% better if you add a friendly wager to the
equation.

Even if it's a mere ten bucks per player, that equates
to four months of competitive gaming and countless
hours of enjoying this sport with the chance to win
upwards of 100 dollars depending on if you split the
pot/how many teams are in your league. You spend
more than that on tickets to an hour and a half movie,
so why not spend it on a third of a year worth of fun?

An alternative (or addition) can be to have a 'Sacko'
punishment, as popularized by the television show
The League, for the loser of the entire league. I was
driving home from work just the other day, and I saw
a huge banner on someone's house that said 'Dave Is
A Loser' in big letters, followed by 'Dave lost his
fantasy football league. Don't be like Dave.' Having a
last-place trophy or punishment could add some
entertainment and enticement to keep up the lively
competition between friends as well.

Now let's break down some basic rules of the game:

I. Number of Teams

In most standard leagues (again, I use the term 'most' because fantasy football is a fully customizable game, so there can be exceptions to the general rules), there are 10-12 teams each year. It means you will play against 9 or 11 of your friends throughout the season. Some leagues can have as little as 6 teams; others can reach as high as 16 teams, but for the most part, and for the logistics of everyone enjoying their fair complement of fantasy players during the year, 10-12 is most common.

II. The Draft

Every league will have a form of a draft where each league participant has the opportunity to select the players they would like on their team for the year. We'll look at *tons* of draft strategy tips in Chapters 2 and 3, as choosing the right players early on can help jumpstart your season.

III. Scoring Types

Tip 8: To know where you stand as the season progresses, ensure you understand which type of scoring is being used in your league - Head-to-Head or Points Only (Total Points Scored).

There are two primary types of scoring systems that can be implemented in your fantasy league. It's crucial to know which one your league is implementing, especially when it comes to the playoffs in your league, as it can help determine who is the higher-ranked team overall. **Head-to-Head** scoring is the most common scoring league type. It entails your fantasy team going up against a different league member's fantasy team each week of the NFL season. At the end of each week, whoever's starting roster earned the most fantasy points is the winner. At the end of the season, your fantasy team will have a record that ranks you in your league (and gives you the potential to go to the playoffs).

In **Points Only** (or Total Points Scored) scoring leagues, you don't play against one specific team each week; instead, your total points are totaled throughout the entire season. The aggregate of points scored with the players you started each week are tallied and whichever league member has the highest number of points at the year's end wins the league title. Again, most leagues are head-to-head, as it gives a more competitive feel to play against your friends week after week.

The Point System

After learning the basic rules behind what's important to look for in your fantasy leagues, let's talk about how the players at each position can get you the points you need to start winning contests like a pro.

I. Running Backs/Wide Receivers/Tight Ends

Most places you read about scoring systems in fantasy football will start with the almighty quarterback position. Instead, to give you a better understanding of *why* the points are scored the way they are, I want to start with the other three offensive positions.

Here's an outline of the statistical categories that score you points and how many to expect for each:

Rushing and Receiving Yards: *0.1 points per 1 yard (or 1 point per 10 yards if that's easier to wrap your head around).*

Every time a player runs the ball or hauls in a reception in a real-life game, the number of yards they accumulate will give your team the corresponding number of points. So, let's say one of your wide receivers (remember, you have at least two on your starting roster) records a catch for 25 yards. Those 25 yards equate to 2.5 fantasy points for your team! Similarly, if one of your running backs runs the ball for 18 yards, you guessed it; 1.8 points are awarded.

<u>Rushing and Receiving Touchdowns</u>: *6 points*

This one is about as straightforward as it gets. Just like in the actual game where a touchdown is six points (that ol' extra point is what makes people think '7 points' initially) when a player catches or runs the ball into the endzone, they are awarded six fantasy points.

Tip 9: Learn the importance of PPR and if your league uses this statistical feature or not - it can make or break a season.

<u>Receptions</u>: *0 points, 0.5 points, or 1 point per reception*

I know, I know. You're probably sitting there wondering why there are three different options for this category. Aren't we going over what happens in standard leagues? Well, your thought process is not wrong; I'll give you that. But as I stated earlier, this is what makes fantasy football such a strategic game if you want it to be; it all depends on your league settings (see *Tip 5*).

One of the most 'overlooked until you play' features for newcomers to fantasy football is the ability of your league to award points when a player makes a catch. Some leagues will call a 'standard' league a league that *doesn't* award points for a catch. For example, if your tight end records five catches for 60 yards, their total amount of points scored will be 6.0 (because they only get points for the yards in this scenario, not the receptions).

However, in other platforms' 'standard' leagues, a reception by a player could count as *half a point*. Looking at that tight end example equates to an additional 2.5 points due to his five catches (a half of a point was awarded for each reception). It brings the player's point total from 6.0 to 8.5 points. Other leagues go even *bigger* and award *one full point* for each catch made by a player. If this were the case, this tight end receives five extra points, bringing the total to 11 points in that game.

As you can see, the importance of whether or not your players are obtaining points for their catches can be a *huge* difference-maker. That tight end could have almost double the points depending on the scoring system implemented. Leagues that grant some value of points for a reception are **called points per reception** leagues (or **PPR**, for those of you who are into acronyms - this is one you will hear all the time). There are half PPR leagues and full PPR leagues pretty regularly. In fact, because of the balance it brings to the different positions, most leagues are now using some version of a PPR format. Just make sure you check your league settings, ask about it, and recheck the rules because this can be crucial when deciding who to select on your team. Assessing where a player's value is the highest based on your league settings and available options can be pivotal throughout your season.

Side Note: Quarterbacks (or any other position player outside of the three talked about in this section) would also receive the same points for performing any of these actions (for example, a mobile quarterback picking up rushing yards).

II. Quarterbacks

Quarterbacks are the players that everyone talks about on and off the football field. Many of the most famous players in sports are the leaders on the turf that air the ball out at an exceedingly high rate each year, making them the epitome of athletic superstardom. And while they do tend to rack up more yards and touchdowns than other positions in the real-life game, fantasy football has found a way to even the playing field with the other athletes in your lineup.

Tip 10: Remember that quarterbacks score points differently than the other offensive positions.

Passing Yards: *0.04 points per 1 yard (or 1 point per 25 yards)*

Fantasy points for passing yards are much harder to come by, as the standard point system is only giving one point for every 25 yards thrown (much lower than the one point per 10 yards rushing or receiving). The quarterback position tends to score still (on average) more points than the other positions, but this scoring system helps balance the values. Also, remember: you only have one quarterback slot for your starting roster, whereas you need multiple of some of the other positions. This further balances the worth of each position on your fantasy team.

Passing Touchdowns: *4 points*

Another way to bring unity to the assortment of points being brought in by each position is by having passing touchdowns count for less. Instead of the regular 6 points offensive players receive for scoring a rushing or receiving touchdown, quarterbacks are limited to just 4 points when they throw for a score through the air.

Interceptions: *-1 or -2 points (depending on the platform)*

Yup. Just when you think it can only go up with scoring, there are some downsides as well. For every interception a quarterback throws, they will lose fantasy points for your team.

Side Note: If any other offensive players were to throw a pass in a game, these pass-scoring rules would also apply to them.

III. Other Scoring Opportunities by Offensive Players

Tip 11: Be cognizant of the ways and number of points you can lose because they are just as important as the ones you can gain.

Fumbles: *-2 points*. We talked about interceptions by quarterbacks, but *any* player with the ball has a chance to fumble it.

Return Touchdowns: *6 points*. This one is something we don't see as often anymore as touchbacks, fair catches, or short returns are the more common occurrences during a kickoff or punt. Nonetheless, if a player you have in your starting lineup happens to take a punt or a kickoff return to the house, they will be awarded the standard six points for their achievement.

Two-Point Conversions: *2 points*. No matter the position (even your quarterback), a player will receive two points for a successful two-point conversion. Points are not generally granted for yards gained during these plays.

Tip 12: Pay attention to players who tend to score points in multiple ways.

As we begin to jump into different strategies in selecting key components for your squad, let's not disregard some of the important aspects of certain positions that could give them a leg up against the competition. If a quarterback runs the ball into the endzone, guess what? *Those* touchdowns count for 6 points, just like the other positions (along with receiving the 1 point per 10 yards rushing). When we talk about getting a half or full point for a reception, isn't there a good chunk of running backs that see regular targets too? And vice versa for receivers who may take the occasional handoff and gain some rushing yards?

It just goes to show when you begin exploring which specific players to choose for your team, understanding their statistical tendencies and how they match up with your league's scoring rules can give you a competitive edge.

IV. Bonus Points for Offensive Players

Ok, ok. These are moving slightly away from general standard league rules. Despite that, they're important to note here because these rules can create unique rewards for spectacular performances.

Tip 13: Encourage your league to add a few bonuses to a few statistical categories.

Some of my personal favorites (and more common ones if bonuses are added in your league) include the following:

Two additional points for a touchdown over 40 yards - this can be a passing, rushing, or receiving touchdown. This long touchdown bonus makes these passing touchdowns now worth a total of 6 points and will turn a long rushing or receiving score into 8 points total.

Two additional points if a player reaches 300 passing yards; four extra points at 400 passing yards - A little additional 'point age' for some outstanding quarterback play.

Two additional points if a player reaches 150 rushing or receiving yards; four extra points at 200 rushing or receiving yards - Same thought process here, but focused on great receiver, back, or tight end play.

Crediting 8 points total for a return touchdown, because they are so rare, or including return yards as a part of your league's point scoring system, are fun bonuses as well.

V. Kickers

Maybe you're wondering how the kickers made it to this game. Quite often, the most overlooked position on the field, in fantasy, they tend to be similarly evaluated, yet sometimes falsely. An efficient kicker can solidify your play week to week (you'd be amazed how many games I've won due to the reliability of a consistent kicker). However, some leagues are starting to do away with the position altogether. In standard leagues, though, where a kicker is generally rostered, this is how their points are accumulated:

Extra Point: *1 point*

If the kicker makes the point after a touchdown is scored, they gain a point themselves.

Field Goals from 0-39 Yards: *3 points*

Field Goals from 40-49 Yards: *4 points*

Field Goals from 50+ yards: *5 points*

Field goals are what makes kickers intriguing. Any shorter field goal (less than 40 yards) is considered a standard, three-point field goal. If it is in the forty-range, kickers are rewarded a bonus point (totaling 4 points) for that field goal. An additional two points are awarded if the boot is 50 yards or more, adding up to a hefty 5 points for just one field goal.

VI. Potential Kicker Point Deductions

Tip 14: Check to see if there are penalties for missed field goals in your league.

One other solution commissioners have started implementing to 'spice up' the kicker slot is to include a penalty for missed field goals. These are pretty variable among the commonly used platforms, but if your league instills a missed kick penalty, this is the popular protocol:

Missed Field Goals from 0-39 Yards: *-2 points*

<u>Missed Field Goals from 40-49 Yards</u>: *-1 point*

No point deduction for missed field goals of 50+ yards

As you can see, the easier the kicks are to make, the steeper the penalty is if they are missed.

VII. Team Defense/Special Teams

Team defense and special teams units (the combination of these two sets of players) is a unique fantasy spot to fill on your team. It is not an individual player, but instead a whole bunch of them all in one slot! They account for specific plays made by anyone on a team's defense or on their special teams. Suppose the team you have in the team defense/special teams slot (also generically called 'team defense' or just plainly 'defense') gets two interceptions and one blocked field goal in one of your weeks; your fantasy team will gain points for those stats. Pretty cool, huh? Here's a walkthrough of the different scenarios that will get your unit points:

<u>Defensive or Special Teams Touchdowns</u>: *3-6 points*

It can range from an interception or fumble return for a touchdown for the defense to a punt, kickoff, or blocked kick return touchdown for the special teams unit. When referring to 'standard' leagues for this specific stat, there is considerable variation among the major fantasy football platforms.

Side Note I know I mentioned earlier in the *'Bonus Points for Offensive Players'* section that punt/kickoff return touchdowns were awarded to the offensive players who got them. Those players are also playing for the special teams unit at the time of their score, so the team defense/special teams slot that the individual touchdown-scorer plays for will *also* accumulate points in this instance.

Interceptions/Fumble Recoveries: *2 points*

When offensive players turn the ball over, they lose points. When defenses create turnovers, they add points to their total.

Sacks: *1 point*

When a defensive player sacks the quarterback, your entire defensive unit is rewarded.

Safeties: *2 points*

This special sack occurs when a quarterback is tackled in their end zone. Defensive units are granted the same quantity of points a real-life team is rewarded for creating this type of play.

Blocked Kicks (Field Goals, Extra Points, or Punts): *2 points*

No matter the kick, if the opposing special team's unit stops it, points are awarded.

VIII. Points Allowed Scoring

Each of the team defense/special teams statistics that were just discussed is thanks to an individual effort by one tremendous competitor. It's great that credit is given to the entire unit for fantasy football purposes (although there are special leagues where you can have individual defensive players on your team, which we'll discuss in Chapter 5). But unfortunately, the collective unit can just as quickly *lose* fantasy points for your team as well.

Tip 15: Realize the number of points your defense/special team's position starts with can decrease as the games progress.

On a football team, the defense's main job is to limit the opposing team from scoring in a given game. Consequently, why not derive some of their fantasy points based on this primary objective? One concept that makes this position incredibly unique is that at the beginning of a game, the team defense *starts* with points that can subsequently be lost as they are scored on throughout an NFL game.

I still remember the first fantasy game I ever played. It was against my best friend (who had set up the league at the time), and right as the opening Sunday games kicked off, he had 10 points already. I was like, *how in the world does he already have that many points? The game's just barely kicked off!* Low and behold, he had his team defense/special teams position entered in his lineup during those early games, and I quickly came to realize that it wasn't worth panicking from the get-go.

Here's a rundown of the typical number of points a team defense can start with and what they can be reduced to as they are scored on in an NFL game. **_PLEASE NOTE_** these values will vary slightly from platform to platform. Points are deducted based on the number of points being scored against your team defense/special teams unit (or the number of points they are *allowing*, hence the wording you will see throughout this section and fantasy platforms):

<u>0 Points Allowed</u>: *10 points*

When the game starts, you will see 10 points automatically awarded to your team defense/special teams (again, depending on the platform). As points are scored on your team throughout the game, this number will decrease.

<u>1-6 Points Allowed</u>: *7 points*

If 1-6 points are allowed by your fantasy defense in the real-life game, your team will be deducted 3 points, leaving your team with 7 points from this specific statistical category.

Side Note: <u>DO NOT FORGET</u> about the points you can *gain* from defensive plays (sacks, turnovers, etc.). Just because 1-6 points were allowed by your defense and you lost 3 points from your total score doesn't mean you have only 7 points total, necessarily. Let's say a few minutes into the game (remember, your defense started the game with 10 points); your defense caused a sack (worth one additional point) which led to a fumble recovery (worth an extra 2 points). It would now put your team defense total scoring at 13 points with barely any time passing! But to add to this scenario, unfortunately, the other team gets the ball back and drives down the field and kicks a field goal; now your team defense has allowed points to be scored in that '1-6 Points Allowed' range (the opposing team's field goal is worth 3 points).

The consequence of that? Your total dropped by 3 points, bringing that 13 down to 10. You see, your' Points Allowed' range that tends to decrease during the game isn't the *only* factor in calculating points for your team defense, as you may recall from the previous section. So even though that *specific* 10-point stat dropped to 7 points when the opposing team kicked that field goal, the other defensive stats (the sack and forced fumble) had already added 3 points to the total. It can be confusing, but understanding what can give you points versus what can take them away is vital in grasping how team defense scoring is implemented.

To limit any further confusion, I created a table that shows the two frames of thinking regarding team defense scoring. The two scoring range examples already provided ('0 Points Allowed' and '1-6 Points Allowed'), and the remaining ones, are listed in this table. The way team defense scoring is presented in the league settings on fantasy platforms (*Tip 5*; I told you it would be beneficial to read them) assumes no other defensive statistical categories (i.e., sacks, interceptions, etc.) are in play. It is what is shown on the left-hand side of this table. On the right, an explanation is given to help you comprehend how your points are being calculated (or, more specifically, *deducted*) while taking all defensive statistical categories into account as the game progresses. Each 'Points Allowed' range can be treated as a 'tier'; as more points are allowed by your team defense throughout the game, you move down another tier. Each tier you move down, more points are deducted from your overall team defense score.

Description of Team Defense Scoring You Will See on Fantasy Platforms	Description to Help Make Sense of Team Defense Scoring
0 Points Allowed: 10 Points	If your team defense allows 0 points to be scored on them, your total team defense fantasy score will not be reduced.
1-6 Points Allowed: 7 Points	If your team defense allows 1-6 points to be scored on them, your total team defense fantasy score will be reduced by 3 additional points.
7-13 Points Allowed: 4 Points	If your team defense allows 7-13 points to be scored on them, your total team defense fantasy score will be

	reduced by 3 additional points.
14-20 Points Allowed: 1 Point	If your team defense allows 14-20 points to be scored on them, your total team defense fantasy score will be reduced by 3 additional points.
21-27 Points Allowed: 0 Points	If your team defense allows 21-27 points to be scored on them, your total team defense fantasy score will be reduced by 1 additional point.
28-34 Points Allowed: -1 Points	If your team defense allows 28-34 points to be scored on them, your total team fantasy defense score will be reduced by 1 additional point.
35+ Points Allowed: -4 Points	If your team defense allows 35 or more points to be scored on them, your total team defense score will be reduced by 3 additional points.

Again, the second column deviates from how you will see this presented on the various fantasy platforms. Still, it is intended to help you understand how many points are being deducted from your team defense's total score.

The uniqueness that the team defense/special teams position can bring to your fantasy squad is incomparable. Pick one that performs well, and it could make the difference for you in any given week. Choose one that does poorly, and you could be watching your opponent trickle past you for the win.

Now that we have learned about which positions make up your roster and some of the basic rules and scoring regulations for these spots, it's time to explore who exactly are the best types of players to select for your team. We will also assess when the best time to choose these individuals is, so they don't get swooped up by someone else in your league. The next two chapters will reveal a plethora of tips and strategies on when to select specific positions and some of the pros and cons to address when choosing a player for your coveted fantasy roster.

Chapter 1 Review

In this chapter, you will learn about the following topics:

- Different positions needed to create your fantasy football team
- Methods to ensure a fun season for everyone in your league
- Specific rules to help understand the logistics of your fantasy football league

- Standard scoring breakdown for all positions
- Additional scoring, bonuses, and penalties that players can accumulate

Chapter 2: Pre-Draft Basics and Logistics

Ahhh, the beloved fantasy football draft. Arguably the biggest day of the football season for fantasy managers, this is where the magic begins. People often treat this as a Super Bowl party-level event. I've been to simple gatherings revolving around draft day, had friends rent out restaurants to hold drafts, and even been on extensive vacations surrounding 'draft weekend.' The atmosphere surrounding this wonderful day marks the beginning of another season of glory, pain, victory, and hopefully not too much frustration for all parties involved.

While there is an entire season to make adjustments and prevail victorious with different roster moves on your team, a successful draft to open your season can give you a much-needed leg-up on the competition. Here are some basic tips to help best understand how to prepare and what to expect from your league's draft.

Types of Drafts

However your league decides to implement your draft, it should be an exciting event that kicks off your fantasy season with a bang! Your league may choose to do your draft live and online on the platform you will be using throughout the season. Others may do a live 'offline' draft, which involves having some sort of physical 'draft board' where you manually write which league member chooses which player for their squad (a little old school, but an added original flare to start your league year). Digitally completing this is a little easier to keep up with - the commissioner will have to manually go back and put every pick in the online platform later if participating in an offline draft - but it's super fun either way.

Tip 16: Draft in person with as many people from your league as you can.

Whether you draft online or offline, though, make sure you get together with your fellow fantasy league managers as it's a true comradery-building kickoff to the season! It will give you a chance to catch some people's strategy right off the bat, and even more importantly, it will allow your trash-talking to begin on Day 1.

I. Snake Drafts

Tip 17: Opt for a snake draft in your league, but if you can't, be aware of what type of draft you'll be participating in.

Before choosing your players, you need to know what *type* of draft you will be a part of. The consensus draft style is what's known as a **snake draft**. To explain this, let's assume there are 12 teams in your fantasy league and you have the 2nd overall pick in when the draft order comes out (usually you won't know this in advance, so it makes it harder to strategize until you're 'on the clock' of the draft). In the first round, you will pick 2nd; however, the draft will *snake* back around and completely flip the draft order in the second round, causing you to now draft second to *last*. Then in the third round, you would get the second pick again, and so on. This type of draft allows for a level of blind fairness amongst all members of your league, even if you have a late-round pick due to no fault of your own. It creates a level playing field for all members drafting and is the main reason snake drafts are the most preferred draft type for standard fantasy leagues.

II. Straight Drafts

Straight drafts follow the same draft method that most professional sports teams use to select players every year. If you have the 2nd pick in this situation, you have that pick in every single round. Obviously, in real-life sports, your draft pick is determined by how poorly/well you performed the previous year, *and* you are selecting players from colleges around the country. Since you won't be doing either of those in your fantasy football draft – you're drafting an entirely new team each season, and it is out of the entire pool of players in the NFL – this isn't deemed as the fairest draft style for standard league play. You tend to see these kinds of drafts implemented more in leagues that are more specialized, outside of the standard ones we have been discussing. We'll talk

about these types of leagues - where you keep players
year after year - in Chapter 5.

III. Auction Drafts

Tip 18: Don't start with an auction draft if you are new to fantasy football.

The last type of draft your league can have is an
auction draft. These are generally for more
advanced fantasy football players but can still be seen
in standard league play. This draft consists of having
the same starting allotment of 'money' (not real
money, but an imaginary currency budget) for each
fantasy manager. And instead of having different
rounds where people draft every few minutes, each
NFL player is 'put up for auction.' Whoever bids the
most money for a player has them on their team for
the year; the caveat here is you have to ensure you
have enough money to obtain all the players you need
for a complete roster. It can make for a *very* timely
process, which is fun for some, but not for all,
depending on your interest and skill level.

Positional and Player Value

The thought of researching anything – never mind a
new hobby - may make many people cringe. Yet, some
basic pre-draft strategies can be rather seamless to

implement when it comes to draft technique, making this 'research project' productive and enjoyable. Whether you're new to the game of football or you're a seasoned fan, these terms and tips will benefit your draft preparedness immensely.

I. ADP

Tip 19: Learn about and use ADP to your advantage, but don't rely solely on it.

The easiest way to research a player's fantasy value is by understanding their **average draft position**, or **ADP**. ADP is a very useful ranking that each player is assigned to interpret where 'experts' think players should be drafted. You can definitely have a love/hate relationship with ADP. On the one hand, it can give fantasy managers - who are unsure of the value they may be getting (or not getting) by drafting a player at a specific time - incredible insight with just one simple number. Sounds fantastic, right? Well, on the other hand, this could also act as a crutch if you have needs at a specific position when your turn comes up in around in your draft.

For example, it's the second round of your draft, and you previously selected one of the league's elite wide receivers in the first round. The next man up on the draft board (according to the ADP rankings next to the player) may be another wide receiver. Should you take him? It's not that having two game-breaking wide receivers is a bad thing – not at all. Instead, it's the significant decrease in your chances of now being able to snag a top running back since you are in the third round without one (running backs tend to be drafted in the top rounds due to their high value – we'll go over that more in Chapter 3).

As you can see, this can be a tough egg to crack, depending on your level of certainty in what you truly need in the round you are currently participating in versus who is available. Part of your decision is about the best available player, but another large part is about the positional need for your overall team. It can be tricky and will vary for all drafts, so we'll dive into some tips on how to go about navigating these waters.

II. Floor vs. Ceiling

A player's **floor** and **ceiling** are two terms you should be familiar with when evaluating potential additions to your team. A floor is known as the lowest amount of points a player will typically score in fantasy football. A ceiling is the opposite; the most points an athlete can regularly attain. You might be thinking to yourself, *huh? How the heck could anyone know the exact range of points someone could get? Can't any player blow up at any time or have a big dud of a game?*

The answer? Absolutely. But these terms can be advantageous in a more general sense to gauge a player's *typical* performance patterns throughout the entire season. The options are high ceiling, high floor, low ceiling, and low floor. Each player can be categorized with some combination of a ceiling and floor that generally assesses their style of play.

Side Note: When you are looking at specific players, there will be no indication of what type of floor or ceiling they have; **this is just a way to categorize a player's typical fantasy value (with the keyword being *typical*).** This categorization can only be determined by a comparison of the average statistics of other players at that position, ADP value, and your own general research based on a specific player's situation on their NFL team.

Here is an example of each:

Tip 20: Aim for high floor/high ceiling combinations for players at the top of the draft; anything else will be a mistake.

High Floor/High Ceiling:

These are most commonly found with some of the higher drafts picks in your league. Take a player that is expected to be drafted in the first round, for example; a reason they are ranked so high is that they, on average, accumulate an abundance of points, even in their bad games (high floor). They also have the potential to get a higher number of points than most other players (and regularly could outperform their floor average) because of their skill level at their position (high ceiling). It could be a player that gets the ball a great deal each game and regularly converts those touches into large amounts of yards, scores, etc. These are the 'top dogs' of your team. They are considered **low-risk, high-reward** players to have on your roster because there is a relatively low risk they will underperform and should reward you with a high number of points on average.

High Floor/Low Ceiling:

The next most consistent category of fantasy players outside of your high floor/high ceiling ones is these guys. They generally score a substantial quantity of points on a regular basis (high floor). Still, with a low ceiling, their potential is pretty limited in getting too many additional points outside their typical floor range.

An excellent example of this sort of player is a running back who gets plenty of carries every game, which leads to an abundance of yards but is limited in the touchdown department. Maybe when his team gets inside the ten-yard line, they substitute in a larger running back to slam in the rock for the score, inherently stealing the ever-so-sought after touchdown. The running back you are vetting still has a heavy workload but is regularly limited by the goal line snubs of another player.

Although these are about as close to 'safe bets' as you can get outside of your few stud players, you generally won't see much more scoring than the high floor you tend to get from them. Still, a comforting style of play to possess on your roster because of the general predictability*. These players are **low-risk, medium-reward** (they give you a nice, consistent number of points each week, but that quota isn't jumping to insanely high levels regularly).

*I use *predictability* lightly here as any player in any week can completely surprise you, good or bad. Fantasy football is an extremely invigorating but wildly frustrating game at times because of its unpredictability. Anything that can give you even the littlest sense of 'regularity' is a win in my book.

Low Floor/High Ceiling:

Players you are evaluating with this type of repertoire are some of the most unpredictable ones in the world of fantasy football. Here, you basically have a player who can either put up a dud of a game or completely blow up your scoreboard, which can be equal parts exciting and frustrating. An example of this type of player may be a wide receiver who doesn't get many catches in a game (maybe 3 or 4 on average). Some days he may total 40 yards from those few catches, and other days he may earn 90 yards and two touchdowns on those same grabs. It is the definition of a gamble in fantasy player selection. An abundance of potential with the high ceiling of churning out points, but wildly inconsistent because of multiple not-so-productive weeks as well. It is the ultimate **high-risk, high-reward** situation.

Tip 21: Ruminate on the combinations of floors and ceilings you would like out of each positional group that you draft and choose players that best fit your style.

Low Floor/Low Ceiling:

By now, you are probably catching on to what these terms mean. And that should be enough to tell you to stay away from people with this combination of a floor and ceiling because there are zero upsides to having them on your squad. Without the potential of getting many points regularly and not a real chance of having an explosive performance either, these are players to avoid—**high-risk, low-reward, not smart.**

III. Mock Drafts

Does all of this make sense so far? If not, it's ok! We will expand on many of these new ideas as we continue to explore this gratifying sport. There is a great deal of information to absorb (mainly because there are so many players), but using these methods in your deliberation when drafting can bring you much success.

Now that you have an idea of ranking fantasy value, who should you draft, and when should you select them? Obviously, the individual players you draft year-to-year will alter draft position based on their prior and projected performances. Still, there is a good amount of strategy involved in making smart overall decisions time and time again come draft time.

Making educated choices will make all the difference regarding the specific positions and the value each of them has over one another, depending on who's available when it's your turn to select a player. A great way to figure a lot of this out in a fun environment is to participate in some **mock drafts** before you participate in your real one.

Tip 22: Participate in a few mock drafts prior to your draft date.

Before your drafts start, your fantasy football platform will have opportunities for you to participate in 'fake drafts,' essentially. You select an online draft you would like to enter (it puts you with a bunch of random people who are also interested in participating), and you will perform a draft. The benefits of being a part of what is known as a mock draft are that you perform the same tasks as you would in your actual draft, but with absolutely zero pressure and stakes. It will help you discover when certain players are being drafted that you may be interested in or who maybe you *should* be targeting based on their consensus popularity. Undoubtedly, not everyone doing a mock draft has expansive knowledge of the game, so take what you notice from others with a grain of salt. Despite that, even the most experienced fantasy football players tend to use mock drafts prior to their actual real-life ones, mainly to assess common trends and values of different players based on their original rankings (and because it's fun, clearly)! Each round of the draft is also timed (you are 'on the clock'), so these practice runs can help you improve your abilities in making ever-so-important decisions under the pressure of time constraints come to your actual draft date.

Definitely do a few of these; don't limit yourself to just one, as doing a handful of these drafts will give you a broader scope of the way they are completed. They don't take long either. You can be half paying attention to a rerun of your favorite sitcom and still make out with some helpful information. And you may enjoy them so much you participate in even more than you initially expected. At the very least, it will get you fired up for your real draft.

IV. Auto-Drafting

Tip 23: DON'T auto-draft your team.

There is an option in every fantasy football league to have the platform you are playing on automatically draft players for you based on an algorithm of value, positions, and available players based on your selection spot in each round. I *highly* suggest you **avoid** using this feature, as convenient as this may sound for a newcomer to the sport. If the idea of choosing a bunch of players to represent your football livelihood sounds daunting the first time around, that's ok.

First and foremost, the draft (as previously stated) is loads of fun. If you slightly research players beforehand (if you are new to the game of football as a whole), you can be the proud possessor of a great fantasy squad. If you decide to wing it and just draft people based on their ADP values presented on the screen for you while you are drafting, you can still end up with as good a team as a 20-year vet (just ask my wife... sigh). Not only that, but it gives you the joy of making the selections yourself, almost like doing your civic duty of voting, in a way. Sure, this analogy may be a stretch, but you can choose a player and toss him to the curb the next day in this situation (something we sometimes wish we could do with said civic duty). But the idea of going out and selecting the person best to represent your wants (in this case, a fantasy football championship) is the way to go.

Second of all, the season is a long one. With the season lasting around four calendar months, there could be a whole slew of new players that you've had to pick up due to a plethora of different reasons, causing you to barely recognize the team you originally drafted. A few years back, I had two of my top three draft picks go down with season-ending injuries in the first few weeks of the season. Between those devastating blows and just a mixture of poor play and movement in and out of my starting roster, I only had *three* players left on my team at the end of the year that I originally drafted. In Chapter 4, we'll talk about how managing your team is the most valuable thing you can do and that drafting is just the beginning step to that process.

Lastly - how *you* manage *your* team down the stretch shows the strengths of a true fantasy football champ, so get out there and draft to the best of your ability - with the help of this book, of course. And don't auto-draft. Treat this as a mandatory meeting at work that you absolutely cannot afford to miss. Except instead of a potentially dull, scary, or pointless event, expect an invigorating one involving friendly competition and a newfound love for an addicting hobby.

Side Note: As stated in this section, you do have the ability to add and drop players that you originally drafted on your initial fantasy team. The draft is your first chance to get the best players possible *before* the season starts, but obviously, different players emerge and underperform as the season gets into full swing. Because of the changes in any given player's real-life performance, your league will have all of the 'available' players (the ones that weren't drafted by you or any of your league mates, also known as **free agents**) on what's called the **waiver wire**. It is an online list of all these remaining players at each of the fantasy football positions. You will also have to give up one of your current players on your roster to choose a different player off the waiver wire. The logistics and strategy behind waiver wire moves throughout the season will be discussed in Chapter 4 in greater detail.

Now that you've done a little bit of research, understand a few terms, and have potentially done a few mock drafts (or at least figured out how to log onto the platform to draft with everyone), it's time to get your season off to a great start! In Chapter 3, we'll evaluate the different rounds of a standard fantasy football draft and discuss which types of players you should be targeting and why.

Chapter 2 Review

In this chapter, you will learn about the following topics:

- Ways to ensure an enjoyable and successful fantasy football draft
- Best type of draft for your specific experience and interest level
- Analysis techniques to determine players' fantasy values prior to your league draft
- Mock drafts and their importance to your pre-draft strategy
- Benefits of selecting your own team

Chapter 3: Draft Strategy: Early Rounds vs. The Crucial 'Rest' of the Draft

The time has come to select your team. You did some mock drafts to brush up on current trends, and you're at a fun location with all of your friends. It's time to show off your draft skills. In the first few rounds of the draft, there is so much excitement! These are the rounds you'll draft the stars that your team will be built around. Yet, selecting great depth for your team later on in the draft can truly make you stand out from the competition. Making excellent choices at each position can be a huge determiner in the success of your overall draft. So, who should you pick? And when? Here are some pointers that can help you make the most informed decisions depending on who is available when it's your time to choose.

The Early Rounds

You have the choice of the top echelon of players at this early stage. If you have the number one pick in your league, your first choice is limitless, but it will be a while before your second one. And even with the last pick in the first round, there are still plenty of studs left to assemble your franchise around; not to mention back-to-back picks (if you select 12th in a standard 12-team league, you will pick first in the following round as the draft snakes back around, remember). What are some things that you can do to ensure you get the most value for the first few players selected for your team?

I. Running Backs

Tip 24: Draft a running back early; even two.

It cannot be stressed enough. A top running back is as valuable as water in a desert. You need a decent amount of them to have a good team, but the number of decent ones available is pretty limited once you get past the top few. There are plenty of wide receivers to choose from (arguably three draftable ones on most NFL teams), and you only need one quarterback and one tight end on your starting roster in a standard league.

Running backs stand out because each NFL team either has one regular starter or a few that share touches. However, your fantasy team needs two, maybe three (depending on your flex position), to **START** on your team alone, not to mention your bench players. Not only that, but outside the top few starting running backs in the league, there is usually a pretty significant drop-off in fantasy production (and an even more significant one outside the top half).

So how the heck are you supposed to lock down the solid running backs? Draft them early, and draft them often. Good players at other positions will be available later on due to the depth of skill for each of them or the quantity needed for your team. Most of the first-round-ranked players in your draft will probably be running backs, with an occasional wide receiver or two sprinkled in.

II. Wide Receivers

Tip 25: If you draft a wide receiver in the first round or two, make sure you feel confident they will be a top player.

Wide receivers are another commonly targeted pick in the early rounds of most drafts. Like running backs, you need at least two of them on your starting roster, with the potential of a third in your FLEX. However, the way they differ from running backs is that there are generally at least two (and often three or four) wide receivers playing on the field on most plays in a real-life NFL game. Whereas, in this same instance, there is typically only one running back lined up in most formations.

A few wide receivers will most likely be chosen in the first round, but generally, they come with the mid-to-late first-round picks. These receivers are expected to dominate on their team, with their quarterbacks constantly getting them the ball to continuously turn into points (catches, yards, and touchdowns). As the second round approaches (and especially once the third round and later come around), you'll start seeing wide receivers taken more regularly. It is because a good deal of the first-rate running backs will be off the board once the initial wave of drafting begins, leaving the wide receiver position as your next biggest need (from a quantity standpoint) on your roster.

The top wide receivers will (and should) go early on in the draft, but don't pass up on a potentially great running back if you're in need just because the ADP of a receiver is higher. Remember always to be attempting to create the best team possible.

III. Tight Ends

Tip 26: Choose a top-tier tight end - or wait.

Tight ends are among the trickiest and most overlooked positions to draft in all of fantasy football. Every year there are two or three tight ends that may emerge as the best receiver on your fantasy squad, but outside of those few, the pickings are slim. If one of those rare tight ends is available and the best value pick in these early rounds, grab them if you like. But what do you do if you choose not to or don't have a chance to get one of those top competitors? Why not wait? The talent difference between those few stellar tight ends and the next batch can be *incredibly* steep, especially considering what you could be giving up to **reach** (a term defined as picking players earlier in the draft than they are projected to go) for a lower-end tight end. The difference in value between the players within that next batch is generally much smaller. The goal with any fantasy team is to have the best balance of positions/players possible, so it's essential to strive for that stability.

Now, maybe drafting a running back in each of the first two rounds is the strategy you decide to go with; or perhaps you find a diamond-in-the-rough tight end or top-grade wide receiver you want to grab because he's the best *value* of player there is when it's your turn to draft. The bottom line is everyone will do something different early on in the draft. Your goal is to capitalize on other's mistakes and secure as complete a team as possible. It will stem greatly from finding players in certain positions that will go away quickly now and waiting on drafting other positions if their value is still high later on in drafts.

The Middle Rounds

I. Quarterbacks

You may be wondering – what about the quarterbacks? Aren't they the player that has the ball every single play? The quarterback position is a crucial part of a football team in real life and in the fantasy world, so shouldn't I have chosen one already?

Tip 27: Wait on drafting a quarterback. As hard as it may be.

I know, I know – quarterbacks are the players who get the most touchdowns and bring all the glory to their teams. There are *always* those quarterbacks you see in the early rounds who had MVP-type stats the year before and seem impossible to pass up. Tons of people in your mock drafts were reaching for a few particular studs on a regular basis. Despite those sentiments, you should wait. Why not shoot for a quarterback with the best *value* instead?

We just discussed how running backs are few and far between. Even though quarterbacks produce more points on average, running backs are generally selected earlier in leagues due to their scarcity and the greater quantity needed on your starting roster. The difference between the third-highest ranked quarterback and the tenth-highest ranked one is *minuscule* compared to those same rankings for running backs.

If a quarterback slated to go in the fifth round of the draft falls a round or two (is still available in the sixth or seventh round), *that's* a solid value pick. If you reach for a big named quarterback too early, though, you may be **hurting the other open spots** on your team; again, especially considering you only need one quarterback on your starting roster.

II. Second-Tier Running Backs, Wide Receivers, and Tight Ends

We talked earlier about the sheer quantity of some of the positions needed for your fantasy football lineup. After you decide on some top players for your starting roster, how do you find additional starters and/or bench players to nicely compliment your team?

Tip 28: Go after players who are targeted a BUNCH.

Drafting a wide receiver who scored ten touchdowns last year sounds impressive, right? But is that number sustainable this year if he did it with only 60 catches? Is there anyone that may take targets from this player this season, or could he start being double-teamed more often? We obviously all want players that score us loads of touchdowns, but some of the best fantasy players are the ones that their quarterbacks look to regularly. These players get consistent opportunities to get the ball in their hands and increase their stats. In PPR leagues, this is even more crucial and can be a true game-changer. And this isn't just a tip for wide receivers; if a running back catches passes frequently out of the backfield, that player's worth may be significantly greater compared to his counterparts.

I had a fantasy matchup a few years back where I decided to start a running back I had selected in the ninth round of the draft (for bench depth, mainly) that I hadn't started this season so far. He hadn't seen the field much that season, but over the previous two games, he saw an average of *eight* targets. Even though those targets didn't turn into much production (just a few catches and no touchdowns), in the upcoming week, he was playing a very weak pass defense, and the primary running back on that specific NFL team was limited with a knee injury. That afterthought of a running back hauled in 10 catches on 15 targets over 100 yards and a touchdown that week for me. The targets paid off and at a great value.

Tip 29: Select a tight end targeted in the red zone.

While this may contradict the previous tip about aiming for players with plenty of opportunities to touch the ball, most tight ends in this part of the draft (presumably, second-tier ones) aren't seeing consistent targets on a per-game basis, but you still need one for your lineup. So, what's the next best thing to do? Select a tight end that is more likely to be targeted when teams get into scoring positions.

As stated earlier, the more touches, the better. *But*, if there are some tight ends available that are a central focal point for their quarterbacks down by the goal line, these touch-limited pass catchers could pay off. There may be some players at other positions that fit this category as well (i.e., running backs subbed in for goal-line touches, wide receivers who don't get the ball often but are looked to more in the red zone). Still, the quantity of better options at these other positions is generally much larger than the tight end position, which only produces a few exceptional players (statistically) each season.

Tip 30: Target a number-one wide receiver on a not-so-good NFL team over an enticing one in a crowded receiver room.

This one can be tough. There could be a wide receiver that pops up during your turn in the draft that you're really excited about and you feel has a chance for a great year. He's a talented wideout in a high-flying offense, with plenty of talented receivers around him and excellent quarterback play. There is also another receiver with a similar ADP who doesn't seem as valuable to you, as the team he is on struggles to do much offensively.

Here's the exciting thing about fantasy football: **volume** - or the number of times a player has a chance to touch the ball - is vital. If the receiver on the loaded offensive team has two other great wideouts ahead of him on the depth chart (making him the WR3 of that team), what are the chances of him having a high volume season in catches, yards, and touchdowns? Does the fact he has to compete on a team that has plenty of mouths to feed hinder his potential to perform at a high level statistically? What about the receiver on the not-so-flashy offense? If he is the clear-cut number one pass catcher (WR1) with little-to-no competition for touches, does that change things? No matter how good the WR3 (and his team) is, think about the sheer volume alone (number of looks from his quarterback) that the WR1 should receive. Quite frankly, if the offense isn't particularly exemplary, they could be behind in plenty of games as well, which could turn into airing the ball out *more often* than not.

Of course, there are exceptions to this rule; every season, there are a few teams that can field three fantasy-relevant receivers. All the same, if you get to these middle rounds of the draft and have to make a decision, it may be easier to snag that WR1 on the mediocre team as the stigma surrounding this player will be poorer overall, but his value should be similar.

Tip 31: Continue adding running back depth to your roster.

It probably sounds familiar to *Tip 24*. You may feel that since you already took two running backs in the early rounds, you don't need to focus on taking any more right away. I'm not saying to disregard ensuring your team is balanced, but even if you already feel you have your starters at the tailback position, keep adding them. Between the backfields that end up being committees (meaning, two running backs on the same team share the carries pretty evenly throughout each game), to the never-ending injuries, along with the goal line touchdown snubs, you'll want to have as many quality running backs as you can to choose from. And it's also worth noting that the worthwhile ones will be gone soon if they aren't already.

Tip 32: Go for players with the best value on the board in these rounds

Chances are you already have some solid skill-position players at this point in your draft, but as you continue to hear: good depth is key to a successful fantasy season. In these middle rounds, try to find great value (the best available players) at some of the positions you are interested in targeting to ensure your team has great quality throughout. Your bench is just as crucial as your starting roster, and at any given moment, you could be relying on them to give your squad the best shot at winning weekly.

The Late Rounds

I. Kickers and Defenses

Kickers and Team Defense/Special Teams are the positions most people do the least research on and care minimally about when it comes to drafting. Quite often, fantasy managers just target whoever the best remaining ones are based on ADP when they feel like selecting these positions in the draft. It may not be the worst plan of action. But is there a more advantageous way to help make certain you get the most out of these positions for the entirety of the season, without sacrificing too many other drafts picks in the process?

Tip 33: Choose a kicker before selecting a defense, preferably with your second to the last pick to close out your draft.

Kickers tend to be the least 'sexy' position in fantasy football. Being that they are only out on the field for a handful of plays, it makes sense. Still, as we discussed in Chapter 1, a consistent kicker can genuinely make or break your team in a given week.

There will be league managers who draft a kicker a few rounds earlier than the recommended second-to-last round to lock in that known long-field-goal-slamming player on an offense that is consistently scoring points (meaning, they'll get that nice extra point for your team multiple times a game too). Others may wait and select them in the last round because they are in the mindset of kickers being a waste of a fantasy football position. Whatever the thought process, there are a good chunk of kickers (on an average year, around eight or ten) that can be a consistent part of your team.

With statistics alone, if you can pass up the top few kickers but not wait until the last round (again, try the second to the final round), you can still lock down one of the top ten kickers, assuming you're in a standard 12-team league. It's definitely worth the effort. I've come from behind in some close matchups due to a long, last-second boot or a five-field goal performance on a Monday night from a steady, reliable kicker on many occasions.

Tip 34: Pick a defense based on their weekly matchup.

You may be thinking that because defenses are on the field more often than kickers, they have the potential to score more points ordinarily. This thought is only partly true. Depending on your league scoring setup for defenses (see the _'Points Allowed Scoring'_ section), it may be pretty hard to get consistent points from that position, though, whereas one quick long field goal out of your kicker can get you a whopping five points.

In standard leagues, most managers are typically drafting one defense. While there are a few projected 'potent' defenses each year that get swooped up before the last round, why not pick a defense that is playing a _poor_ offense each week? There are bound to be around 50% of the team defense/special teams available on the waiver wire (assuming a 12-team league and each team only chooses one defense) every week, leaving you plenty of options to choose from. Draft a defense you see having a relatively easy beginning-of-the-season schedule, but don't be scared to pick up a different defense with a better matchup in later weeks. Also - don't be afraid to drop that defense the following week for the next best matchup you find. Other people in your league may become complacent with their 'great' defenses, but even the best defenses could have to face Patrick Mahomes some weeks.

II. Sleepers

Sleepers are another fun adventure in fantasy football. These types of recruits can make you look like the Road Runner of your draft, or the Wile E. Coyote, depending on how the results pan out. Sleepers are defined as players who are not anticipated to get selected very early (not expected to be in the tops at their position). Still, you have an 'inkling' based on research/team situation/a gut feeling (all super-scientific reasonings, of course) that they will overperform their ADP.

Tip 35: Optimize your chances of picking a solid, late-round sleeper in your draft by incorporating them into your preseason research.

Every year, a lucky few select that random wide receiver in the last few rounds of the draft who everyone says, *why would you pick him?* Come to find out a few weeks later that late-round flyer is outperforming your top-drafted pass catcher. However, the opposite of this situation also happens extremely often. Suppose you're drafting someone the majority of others don't expect to perform very well throughout the season. In that case, you won't be giving up too much to select them in your draft (a low-risk, potentially high-reward situation if it pans out). If you're researching players or you're participating in some mock drafts prior to the season, make a note of a few potential sleepers you may target late in drafts if they are still available.

Vital Tips for All Stages of the Draft

Tip 36: Be cautious with rookies.

Each season, there are a few 'hot' rookies who are valued very high in drafts. By no means am I saying not to select them; some players *do* explode onto the scene each season (ala Saquon Barkley, 2018). But college football results don't automatically translate to the pros. Especially when you are looking for a solid starter; now, this thought process could be much riskier. Have a solid backup plan with a few other players to toggle through on your team just in case this strategy doesn't pan out as nicely as projected.

I drafted a 'top projected' rookie running back with my *first-round* pick one year. Again, these can pan out great some seasons as rookie running backs frequently have the opportunity and sheer talent to hit the ground running in Week 1. Unfortunately, that wasn't the case in my particular instance. He had a few good weeks statistically and then just didn't see the ball much due to irrelevant game script: calling for more throws downfield and fewer running back touches. He was a first-round talent for sure but not used that way in the system he was drafted into, which negatively affected his fantasy value.

Tip 37: Contemplate 'intra-team' competition.

What if you already have a top wide receiver from a specific team, and now the WR2 (the second wide receiver) of that _same_ team falls into your lap? Despite that receiver potentially being a great selection, do you see _both_ receivers having great fantasy days consistently? Do ten catches, 100 yards, and a touchdown seem feasible for two wide receivers sharing throws from the same quarterback every week? There are definitely some exceptions to this, but overall, it may be wiser to trend towards two players at the same position on different teams. It can also apply to choosing running backs. Many people flock to the most electrifying runners, but what if they are sharing the field in a committee? It means they aren't on the field as often. If a running back is on a team with no other competition and gets 20 touches a game, their odds for getting you a higher point total are much greater.

Tip 38: Don't get bogged down by bye weeks.

While it's not ideal for half of your team to have a Week 8 bye, just remember - it's only one week. A large part of your role as team manager will be finding an assortment of different players on the waiver wire to fill in gaps due to injuries and underperforming players throughout the season. Bye weeks are definitely something to have in the back of your mind; however, don't let them deter you from picking a great valuable player. As I mentioned about my injury-plagued season, your team may look a great deal different as bye weeks approach, so don't get caught up in these early on.

Tip 39: Consider what you're passing up before making a final decision on which player to choose.

Were you thinking about grabbing that incredible quarterback in the fourth round or your second wide receiver in the third? You know the upside of snagging a top quarterback or a pair of wide receivers, but what could you be giving up to get these players? Maybe now it's too difficult to find a complementary running back or a solid asset for your flex position. Every time you make a decision in your draft, don't just think of what you're getting, but also consider what you're giving up.

It is arguably the most important tip when it comes to your fantasy league draft. While everyone in your league will have the same position quantities on their starting rosters, your bench players can be made up of _any_ positions available. Getting depth, but good quality depth is a crucial gamechanger in your draft. Numbers (quantity) at specific positions are vital, but getting the best (quality) players at each position can only be attained if you are selecting these players at the perfect time in the draft. Ensure you use the tips in this chapter, along with any of your own research on current players, to make the best decisions possible for the timing of your draft selections.

With all of that being said, this is much easier said than done. I've played fantasy football for upwards of two decades and have seen fantasy teams rise to the top and others just be obliterated entirely. Even if you do everything perfectly in the draft (which honestly, you won't truly know until the season is over) and your outlook is top-notch, many factors can derail your dreams of an amazing season. Injuries, players underperforming, your opponent's players overperforming; the list goes on. But this is why managing your team throughout the season is arguably *more* crucial than the opening draft.

Tip 40: Understand the importance of 'handcuffs' but don't make it your mission to ensure they are on your team.

It is one tip that is heavily debated in the fantasy football community. **Handcuffs** are a star player's direct backup that you keep on your team if that player has to miss a fair amount of time due to an injury/suspension/etc. For example, let's say your number one pick is an amazing running back that touches the ball upwards of 25 times per game, constantly rolling in points for your squad. If he suddenly suffers a season-ending injury, but you have his handcuff (his backup), you have the guy that will step right up in his place. That should lead to pretty similar production, right?

It is more of an 'awareness' type of tip in that just because you have those specific circumstances unfold doesn't mean the logic will follow. There are plenty of teams that love to get their backs the ball 20-25 times

74

a game. If you don't have a guy that can produce the way the starter can, though (which assumingly most teams don't since they are the backup after all), it may not be a simple plug-and-play for your fantasy needs.

Contrary to this point, there are offenses with great systems in place that can help all of their runners succeed. Some backups have starting potential and can shine in their own right if given a chance. But think about this; *every* running back has a backup, and *every* runner has the potential to have a season-ending injury. So, if you are sold on drafting a handcuff for your roster, is it vital that the player be one of *your* starters' backups? Not necessarily. A good handcuff is someone who has the potential to break out if given a chance. Since you have no idea what the 'chance' could be, it is pretty fair game that *any* team's backup would suffice. There are other circumstances where a backup may play more: poor play by the starter, a suspension, a split committee of running backs in general (which technically isn't a handcuff situation since there isn't necessarily a clear RB1 in that situation); but these situations are just as unpredictable.

Interestingly, many *pro-handcuff* thinkers will say this is to ensure low risk if a starter goes down on your team. Yet, arguably *anti-handcuff* thinkers say it could easily be the opposite, in that the player is going to take up a valuable spot on your bench. That may seem like no big deal, but if this person never steps into a large enough role on the football field, they could be taking a spot from another potential great bench player that you actually use for the entire year! (See previous *Tip 39* to realize the impact of that decision). A fascinating risk versus reward situation comes into play with this type of player in the draft, so be sure to incorporate your thoughts on specific handcuffs into your draft strategy. Whether you take a chance that you find a diamond in the rough or you avoid them altogether.

___Tip 41: Always think at least one step ahead as players come off the draft board much quicker than you may expect. However, don't be deterred if who you want isn't available any longer; have multiple options.___

Everyone's strategy will be different in drafts, especially early on. You may have a pretty early pick in the first round, but by the time your turn comes around in Round 2, the few players you had in mind were swooped up by your opponents. Now what? It's your turn to pick, but the players you invested all of your excitement in are off the board!

Because of this exact situation (which will happen several times no matter *how* strategically you plan), you should always be thinking more than one step ahead. I know this sounds pretty complicated, especially if you are new to the game of football as a whole. However, it is easier than it seems. For instance, you may have come into the draft knowing that you wanted to pick a running back in the first round. Yet, if you end up with the 10th pick in a 12-team league, maybe you shift your strategy because you know when your turn 'snakes' back around, there are a few solid options of running backs still available. Which, in turn, could give you the ability to grab that stud wide receiver with your first pick, who will be swooped up if you don't take him now. It gives you a top wide receiver while still being able to grab a top-tier running back shortly after with your second pick.

Another scenario: it's later on in the draft, let's say the sixth or seventh round. You already have a handful of presumptive all-stars on your roster, but you need to continue to build some depth. You are waiting your turn patiently and have a particular running back you have been eyeing to add to your talented squad. Should you just sit there and hope that person falls in your lap? What if you *just* had your turn drafting? Chances are, someone else has their eye on that runner as well and will scoop him up before you have a chance. So don't limit yourself to just one future player; expand your thought process.

Having a *handful* of options you are interested in adding is vital. Keeping an eye on how long to wait to draft them versus not wanting them to get swooped out of your reach in an earlier round than you anticipated is not a fun tightrope to walk while you're debating who to add to your roster. There is even a queue box in most fantasy football platforms that allows you to keep track of players that you are interested in potentially adding in the future, so you don't forget any of your thoughts mid-draft. Use this; it can be beneficial. Don't limit your options and get a jump on the other league contenders by planning a few steps ahead, so you don't cave into the pressure once you're on the clock in the draft.

Tip 42: Watch out for position runs and adjust your strategy accordingly if you see one of these occurring.

You are all set. You have taken these first few drafting tips to heart and have your strategy (and some backup ones) all planned out, even if some of your top players are taken before you can snag them. You're feeling confident, right? Well, what if you were holding off a few more rounds to draft your mid-level tight end, but suddenly you start seeing other members of your league go on a tight end drafting spree, pick after pick? You didn't want to choose your tight end yet, and the ADP shows you shouldn't have to for a while, but if you wait any longer, there may not be any usable ones for your roster!

It is a common occurrence (or hindrance, if we're being honest) known as a **position run** in fantasy football drafts. As I mentioned earlier about unpredictability, you can have every backup plan you could ever imagine dreamed up. Still, the minute a position run takes place, you have to make a swift decision that can ultimately skew your entire draft process. Do you follow along suit with some of the others that are jumping on this trend to ensure you get your guy? Or do you hold out and hope that the tight end you were eyeing stays available and the position run ends before they get to him? Or do you just ride it out and hope there's another tight end open when this run ends that meet your requirements? Another organized person's worst nightmare, but something to definitely keep an eye out for to avoid being thrown for a complete loop during your draft.

Tip 43: Drafting isn't everything; managing your team throughout the season is.

I know I probably sound like a broken record with my continual reiteration of this point. It may seem like your draft is the most crucial piece of the puzzle at the time, but in the end, it could be just a blip on your radar. It doesn't mean auto-drafting is the right answer; draft strategy is still an important part of a championship season, as you can see from the last two chapters. But often, your lineup may look _completely different_ by the end of the season, and you may have players you never expected carrying your roster to victory.

The most important thing in fantasy football is to actively manage your team week-to-week to ensure you are giving yourself the best chance to win. Pay attention to those dreaded injuries and bye weeks as the season progresses, and keep fresh eyes out for any hot commodities to increase the strength of your team. All it takes is a few bad games in a row to start second-guessing that stud wide receiver you selected in the early rounds of the draft. Don't get stuck on a player that's underperforming just because they were rated high at the beginning of the season; this could easily prevent you from securing those bragging rights over your friends come December. Fantasy football is a roller coaster ride. That's the beauty and the beast of this beloved game.

Chapter 3 Review

In this chapter, you will learn about the following topics:

- Key qualities and positional groups to watch for in early-round fantasy football draft picks
- Options and decision-making processes for selecting players in the middle rounds of your league draft
- Late round target positions and techniques
- Draft strategies to focus on improving the depth and longevity of your roster
- Helpful approaches to ensure your team choices are not limited
- Specific statistical categories to better prepare your selection process

Chapter 4: Managing Your Team: Your New Obsession

Well, that was quite a bit of information to digest. Between scoring systems, league types, and draft strategies, what else could there be to know? Want to hear the craziest thing? You've made it through three chapters of this book, and we haven't even begun to talk about what to do *during* the season. While you could potentially only be taking a few days of learning the game and drafting your team, addressing the other four months or so of your newfound hobby may be the most critical task of all. Don't worry, though; figuring how to 'take care of your new baby' can be loads of fun and will give you the ultimate satisfaction that comes with a thriving fantasy football franchise.

__Tip 44: Enjoy the hobby of managing your fantasy team; don't neglect it just because things aren't going your way. Don't be THAT league mate.__

As mentioned in *Tip 43*, managing your team is the most vital part of finding success in this sport. You wouldn't research which vegetable seeds you were interested in growing, plant them in the ground, and then neglect to water them regularly, would you? No, because in the end, you want the best vegetables that can be produced! The same thing applies to your fantasy squad; you have researched how to have a successful draft, chosen a solid team, and now have to tend to your 'garden' of players to reap the ultimate benefits. Even if after a few weeks your team is not performing as well as you would have hoped, *don't* abandon ship.

First off, a season can change with one quick injury, one benching of a player, or an opponent with an unfortunate bye week, so keep the faith. Also, this chapter will go over the diverse array of options you have to ultimately improve, maintain, and lead your team to its ultimate goal: a league championship. Therefore, see the season through. Plus, you don't want to be the team that everyone else in the league deems as an easy victory because you gave up. Play spoiler and take down a top team whether it does anything for your playoff hopes or not. Because while it may not get you to the championship, it could *easily* prevent your opponent from grabbing that first-place trophy in the end. And if for none of those reasons, at least play it out so you won't have to endure the last place punishment, like having your head shaved. True story: I definitely had fun shaving my friend's long, golden locks off one year when she dropped to the bottom of the league. I know your instinct is to feel super sorry for her, but everyone agreed on the punishment before the season started, no matter who the last-place finisher was. So, beware! The one in twelve chance you'll be last place will dwindle much more if you just try your best; because chances are there will be some poor sap in your league who doesn't.

Waiver Wire Types

The waiver wire is a magical place you may end up spending countless hours searching for the next great addition to your lackluster lineup week after week. Even if your team has been killing it overall, there is *always* room for improvement. Need a reminder on what waivers (the waiver wire) are? Simply put, players on the waiver wire (known as free agents) are not currently owned by any fantasy manager in your league.

Tip 45: If you only do one thing right in fantasy football, it should be making great moves on the waiver wire throughout the season.

Aren't the free agents from the waiver wire the players who weren't good enough to be selected in the draft? In short, not necessarily. The value of players chosen in the last few rounds could be comparable to those left on the waivers directly after the draft concludes. But to really bring home this point, and the more accurate way to answer this question is: *not at first*. There is a great deal of potential for players not drafted to have an increased fantasy role as the season progresses. Also, some of your fellow league mates may drop a player onto waivers that they initially drafted at some point during the season, making them available for pickup by any of the other teams in your league. We'll go over the different scenarios of how, when, and why to make additions to your team off the waiver wire as we dive into this chapter. Let's start, though, by defining the types of waiver wires your league can have.

Side Note: The purpose of this section is to give you a general overview of the common styles of waiver wire setups. ***HOWEVER,*** be sure to read over your league rules to get a better idea of the _specifics_ related to your individual league and the platform you are using to play on. There can be slight disparities in waiver rules from platform to platform, and they may include variation from what you see here. Follow up with your commissioner to alleviate any confusion as well.

Tip 46: Make sure you know which waiver claim priority system is in place in your fantasy league.

There are multiple options of types of waiver rules a league can abide by. Make it your mission to figure out what order your league has for selecting players off waivers (known as the priority system for claiming free agents). Most fantasy football platforms have some variation of the same waiver wire types; I'll use the terminology from one of these popular platforms to describe each.

Side Note: As stated earlier, to add a free agent off the waiver wire to your roster, you MUST get rid of someone from your current team to make room for your new addition. That's why not only is it vital you understand *how* waivers work, but also the impact they can have on your 'new' team.

I. Standard Waiver Priority

There are a handful of 'standard' types of waiver claim systems (I know, I know; these multiple 'standard' options are getting old) with similar structures but different overall details.

Tip 47: If your league uses a variation of a standard wavier priority, make sure you are clear on how it is implemented to ensure you're able to strategize who you choose off of waivers properly.

Continual Rolling List:

In this type of waiver claim priority system, the waiver order is set from the minute your draft ends. The person who drafted last in your live draft gets the first waiver priority (and the person who drafted first gets the last waiver priority). From there, every time a fantasy league member makes a waiver claim; they fall to last on the priority list, with this order staying the same (and continually rolling) throughout the entirety of the season.

Reverse Order of Standings:

Similar to the continual rolling list, the initial waiver claim for the season is given to the last person in your league's initial draft order. However, the difference from there is the waivers each week change based on how well each fantasy manager's team performs. So if my team, for example, had the least amount of points in Week 4, I would get first dibs on the waiver wire in Week 5 (and the person who scored the second least amount of points gets the second waiver priority, and so on). This changes after each week, basically prioritizing the team who performed the worst (reverse order of standings) the week prior.

Weekly Rolling List Based on Standings:

The weekly rolling list is a blend of the previous two waiver types. After making a claim, the fantasy manager falls to last on the priority list (just like in the continual rolling list), but initial precedence goes to the team with the least amount of points each week (identical to the reverse order of standings method).

Hang on, though. Just because you put in a 'claim' for a player on the waiver wire and have first priority doesn't mean you get that free agent that exact minute you place the request. There is what's known as the **processing period**, which, depending on league settings, occurs once a week at some point before the first NFL games start.

Here's a fairly standard example of this: Fantasy managers in your league have from the beginning of the NFL games each week (assumingly Sunday) until early Wednesday morning (3 am EST/12 am PST) to put into the system the player they would like to claim. It gives team managers a few days to decide who they want to add and a few days to figure out how to use any they successfully add before the upcoming games. Any free agent who isn't taken off of waivers during this processing period can be added to a team without waiting or priority in most standard leagues prior to the upcoming games.

Side Note: If a player is *released* from a team during the week, but *after* the initial waiver period, some leagues will place this player on a 'waiver period,' which can last around 24-48 hours in most leagues. After a player is released, he cannot be added to any team for 24-48 hours (assumingly giving everyone fair time to see the player is available to be added). But this is only if a player has been released; if a player has been on the waiver wire for some time, they are generally able to be snagged immediately, as long as the processing period has concluded, in most standard leagues.

I've played in many leagues that don't have this additional waiver period for released players after the original waiver claim priority has run its course for the week, as it seems plenty fair enough to many. Basically, the thinking here is: you had your chance to add and drop people during the processing period (giving league members plenty of time to make decisions), so go grab whoever you want, whenever you want after that resets.

Understanding what priority you have on the waiver wire and when you'll have it again is very important if you are trying to pick up multiple players during the same waiver period, which you are absolutely able to do in any week. Deciding who to acquire first may throw a wrench in your plans on being able to add the other free agents you're eyeing. Will the person you were trying to choose as your second pickup of the week still be there if you wait that long to snag him? Or should you switch him to being your first priority to claim off waivers? These are all strategies to keep in mind depending on the type of standard waiver priority you have.

II. Free Agent Acquisition Budget (FAAB) Waiver Priority

Tip 48: Opt for a FAAB waiver claim priority system if you can; it is hands down the most strategic (and fun) waiver wire method.

Suppose you don't have the **FAAB** system in place in your league (also referred to as Free Agent Budget or FAB); you are truly missing out. Want to really feel like you are the general manager of a team? How about deciding who you can pick up but on a (fake) budget? At the beginning of the season, each league manager is 'given' a set amount of money (not real money). This number is often 100 dollars - or some even amount divisible by 10 – and it is used to bid on players from the waiver wire during the processing period throughout the season. Each week, fantasy managers will place a *blind* bid on free agents during the processing period. Yes, that means you don't know *if* or *how much* other members of your league bid on the same player. After the processing period comes to a close, the person who bids the most money gets the free agent added to their roster (and their 'money' is deducted from their allotted budget).

But, if you use up all of your money before the year wraps up, you will only be able to claim players during this waiver period if no one else bids on them. Suppose your waiver priority period ends on Wednesday morning, but no one picked up that running back you had been eyeing on waivers. You can then pick him up for 'free' at any time before the cutoff for the next week's waivers (more on the cutoff options shortly). And just like in the standard waivers, if you decide to select more than one player to try to add off of waivers in the same week, the priority in which you organize the free agents, and the amount of money you bid on them should be chosen wisely.

III. No Waiver Priority

The nice thing about this being a 'fantasy' game is that the rules can be bent, changed, and even disregarded altogether if that's what the members of the league all want. I've played in a league for a few years where there are literally no waiver rules at all. You can pick up a player one minute and toss them to the curb the next, the only exception being a player who is currently playing *live* and in your starting lineup, as they would be actively accumulating you points and locked into place for that week. But the minute the game ends, if you see a more enticing player on waivers, you can get rid of that guy for the new one.

You may be wondering why anyone would want to deal with this chaos when there are so many fairer ways to go about having balance throughout the season. I can tell you that in the particular league that disregards the waiver policy that I am a part of, it's because the members feel it is fair this way. All of the members in this league are glued to their televisions on Sundays, watching every play in every game that their eyes can possibly absorb. Consequently, the way they see it: you should all be watching all of these games anyway, so first come, first serve. I don't necessarily agree with this sentiment as that is obviously not everyone's circumstances. Still, being that I'm in multiple leagues, it does give for an extra rapid-fire decision-making edge to that specific one. If you hesitate on picking up that backup running back who just lunged in for his third touchdown of the day in leagues with no waiver priority, someone else will scoop him up before you can blink.

Tip 49: If your commissioner wants input on when to make the cutoff for the waiver claim period, recommend it be at the beginning of the games for the specific player.

We've been talking a lot about how to obtain players off of waivers and when you should expect to be able to perform this action prior to the next week's games. When does the period for picking up free agents (assuming there is some sort of waiver system in place) lock up for the week, though? After the processing period ends (again, usually midweek), you can't just pick up players during the middle of a

Sunday game with a waiver priority order in place, right?

Again, unless there is no waiver wire priority, your commissioner has the ability to alter this a bit:

Option 1: *No players are allowed to be picked up off waivers after the kickoff to the week's first game (usually the Thursday night game).*

This one is a little harsh in that there is only one game on Thursdays (so only two teams play); you may be trying to figure out how to replace some people later on in the week, making this a little premature of a waiver cutoff. This option is not commonly used.

Option 2: *No players are allowed to be picked up off waivers after kickoff to the early Sunday games.*

It is the standard-setting in most leagues and one that ensures no one can pick up players at the start of the majority of the games for the week.

Option 3: *Players are allowed to be picked up off waivers up until kickoff of the specific player's game.*

It is my favorite option as it entices more strategic thinking on different league members' parts. Plenty of people won't agree with me on this one as many say this is a case of *what if I can't watch the games on Sunday?* I see it as a pros outweighing the cons situation. If a player in the late Sunday games (or even the Monday night game) is ruled out late in the day (you will be amazed how many 'game-time decisions' won't go your way in fantasy football), you can snag a quick replacement off the waiver wire, but only if there is one that *also* hasn't played yet already. Therefore, the choices will be limited, and you still have to decide who to get rid of (or if it's worth it) if this situation arises, so it's not a sure-fire option by any means. And you wouldn't have to be necessarily watching the games, but instead, briefly checking your lineup to determine your player's fate before his game's commencement.

Reasons for Targeting Players on Waivers

In case this section has been confusing so far, that's ok. This imaginary 'wire' that holds all of the available players to potentially add to your team comes with an array of options. There are also many terms we've thrown out there that describe the waiver wire: waivers, waiver claim priority system, a claim, waiver priority, free agents... you get the point. If any term has *that* many names for it, it's got to be necessary, right? The main point of that section was to give you the tools to figure out which of these waiver systems your league most relates so that you can effectively strategize who you claim based on when it's your turn to do so. Your league settings will discuss any other specifics related to waiver priority, so don't forget to glance at that before you get too deep into the season.

When we discuss what sorts of free agents you should be looking for to beef up your current roster, some of the previous tips may flash into your mind from the good ol' drafting section of this book; and if you think about it, that makes total sense. If the person you drafted isn't panning out to be what you thought, your strategy for finding new players – now that part of the season has come and gone – could be similar. Maybe that wide receiver you drafted didn't end up getting too many targets the first few games, but there's a great free agent available who has been receiving great volume thus far. It is one great example of many that we'll jump into in this section.

I. Boom or Bust

Boom and **bust** have significant meanings in the world of fantasy football performance value. Sort of like the floor versus ceiling conversation from Chapter 2, certain players have tendencies to perform very well or completely horribly on a not-so-consistent basis. These are referred to as boom or bust players.

One year I had a wide receiver (who I drafted in the fourth round) who ended the season as the 12th best receiver in total fantasy points. Not bad; I got a top 12 wideout in the fourth round. What this number doesn't show, however, is *how* these points were accumulated. The first two weeks weren't bad for me; he had 15 and followed that with 18 points. The week after that, he had a bit of a stinker, with only 6 points. In the next game, he had FORTY-TWO points. Yes, you read that large text correctly. However, the ensuing weeks played out like this: 18, 4, 31, 7, 11… you can see the trend.

Each week these boom or bust players have the potential to *boom*, meaning, get an absolute plethora of points (a high ceiling, if you will). Still, they also have just as likely a chance (or sometimes even more of one) to *bust* or not get many points at all, equating to a low potential floor as well.

We talked about this high-risk, high-reward type of player in the pre-draft section of this book. The difference here is you can evaluate these kinds of players and their statistical trends in their *current* season, giving you the ability to avoid them easier than you could in drafts.

Tip 50: Avoid boom or bust players on the waiver wire for long-term options.

If you have drafted a guy like this on your team, it is tough to bench him due to his potential upside as a fantasy player. Imagine being the guy who has a player with double the amount of points as the rest of the players on the team, but he's sitting on your bench? I definitely felt erratic for most of the season with that fourth-round receiver in my starting lineup, which was incredibly awful for about half of the games. The good news here, though, is you have the ability to avoid these types of players on the waiver wire. No matter how enticing they may be because of their upside weeks, the headaches that ensue the alternative weeks will make it hard to sleep at night. The only exception here is if you are picking the player up for just a short stint on your roster.

II. Bye Weeks

Tip 51: Try to plan a few weeks ahead for bye week absences if you need the waiver wire to add the depth.

If you know you have a rough week or two coming up because of byes, make sure you're constantly glancing at the waiver wire for any potential fill-ins. And really, you should be planning a week or two ahead for bye weeks even if you're not actively diving into the waiver wire; you never know if those bench players will be healthy, good enough, etc., to replace your starters. Plus, there may be better options from the free agent pool that pop up. I did mention in *Tip 38* not to sweat too much about bye weeks during the draft, but during in-season play, it's quite a different story. If you come across some rougher weeks with multiple starters on byes, definitely plan a few weeks out to try to come up with some answers pre-emptively.

III. Injuries

Injuries will probably be the most frustrating, season-changing part of fantasy football every single year you play. Maybe you'll get lucky and not have your number one draft pick go down with a season-ending injury in the first ten minutes of Week 1 like I did a few years back (yea, I don't want to talk about that season). But even if the worst *doesn't* happen, it never ceases to amaze people how much even small injuries can shock your fantasy world.

If a player that was labeled as 'questionable' going into the week (don't even get me started with how frustrating that term is from a fantasy perspective...) but is cleared to play by game-time, it doesn't mean they will see their usual number of snaps. Maybe they have limited reps because of their injury. And what about one of your starters dropping to the turf mid-game? There's nothing you can do except sit back and cringe as your lineup is locked with the people you decided to start pre-game. You'll just have to take the hit and hope he's back on his feet in due time. Even a minor injury that causes a player to miss just a game or two may be too long to wait in an 'every win counts' fantasy season. That's why it's essential to truly study and dig into the waivers so you can salvage as much depth for your team as you can.

Tip 52: Just because a starter went down with an injury doesn't mean his backup is the best waiver add.

A starter's backup can absolutely be a monster add-off waivers if they can produce close to the way the starter can. Yet, how many times have you seen a backup step right in and be the guy the starter was, statistically? It is an extension on the handcuff conversation from Chapter 3, except you wouldn't already have this player on your roster. Know that this is an option (and one that is better than nothing), but if there is another free agent from the waiver wire at

that same position that you like better, don't hesitate
to add them instead. Your goal is to score as many
points as possible, so pick the players you feel will do
that.

Tip 53: If you are in a FAAB waiver system, bet more of your budget than you would typically to claim a solid backup for your injured starter.

Here's a scenario: your star running back, who you
chose in the first round of the draft, has been a stud
for your fantasy team through the first five weeks of
the season. Except in Week 6, he goes down with a
season-ending injury. Now what? That was your *first-
round* selection; how can your team recover from
that? The waiver wire is a great place to start.

If you're in a standard waiver wire system in this
scenario, shoot for someone (or even a few players)
you think would be a great fill-in for your injured star,
and continue to prowl the free-agent list each week if
your first choice doesn't pan out. Undeniably, it will
be tough to find someone to replace such a high-
quality player (chances are, you probably will have to
settle for a lesser player), but you can still find some
good talent if you're savvy.

However, if you're in a FAAB waiver system, this is
where strategy becomes crucial. Now you have to
spend money from your $100 budget to try and
replace your star; that's going to be tough to figure out
how much is worth using to try and salvage that

important roster spot. Whether you go after your star running back's backup on waivers (if available), or one from another NFL team (currently on the waiver wire) happens to emerge as someone who is favored to get more touches in the coming weeks and looks to be a great potential addition, you need to find a real prospect who can help fill the injury void on your team. How much should you bid on that player in this instance? As you know, he will be in high demand by other members of your league, but you feel you may need him to save your season?

In short, pony up the money if you really feel that this can be your guy. If you're not feeling super confident and you've seen a few other players emerge with comparable attributes over the previous weeks in similar circumstances, don't go crazy. But you obviously need to find some talent fast. If you feel you may have to go with a different running back week after week for a bit, be careful with your money; but if you feel like you've found your guy, don't be scared to take a chunk out of your budget to ensure you win the claim for him.

IV. More Tips for Value Waiver Adds

Tip 54: You can pick up a free agent for just a week, especially if the matchup is impressive.

What if you come across a wide receiver on waivers that tends to have a high ceiling but a pretty low overall floor (a boom or bust player) when he plays weak pass defenses? This week that receiver just so happens to play the *worst* team against the pass. Should you scoop him up even if you toss him back to waivers the week after because he has tough matchups following this game? Absolutely. As long as you feel you have another disposable player to get rid of in place of this potential one-week breakout, go for it.

Avoid boom or bust players on waivers for long-term strategy (like *Tip 50* says), but if you are heading into a player claim *knowing* it's just for a week, it can be a great move. Fantasy football may seem like a long season, but every single game counts. This is a big step to solidifying a 'W' for that week, don't get attached to 'your' players. Use them when they're needed and move on when they aren't.

Tip 55: Be sure to do a risk/reward analysis when exchanging players on waivers.

Make sure you believe the person you are picking up off waivers is better for your situation than the player you are getting rid of because there's no guarantee you can get that other player back. Remember: you picked the player you are debating about getting rid of first. I'm not saying things don't change because they do, *all the time* throughout a long football season. Do your best, though, to be sure the new player's 'pros' outweigh the old player's 'cons' and feel as confident as you can about your decision.

Tip 56: If a great player is available at a position you already have solid depth in, make a run at them anyway.

Let's say your team is off to a strong start, and you have a handful of great players (even on your bench) that you feel can take you a long way. Why put any thought into waivers? As you can see from all of the scenarios that can pop up (injuries, bye weeks, real-life benching, etc.), your team is never really completely finalized. If a player emerges as someone who would be an asset to any fantasy roster - even if you already have good depth at that position - it can only make your team stronger to add them. As long as the 'hot' player has more upside than a person on your bench, and even if you don't end up using him regularly, you can never have too many stars. Also, realize that if you don't snag that player, someone else in your league will, and chances are you _will_ play against them at some point.

Tip 57: Watch out for injury-prone players on waivers.

Injury-prone players are a common waiver wire guilty pleasure. These are the types of players who play 'lights out' football most of the time they are on the field. The problem with this is: you never know when they will or won't see the field. If a player always seems to be battling some sort of injury, is pulled regularly from drives during games, or has a track record of consistently missing multiple weeks at a time each season, they are classified as an injury-prone player. It's hard to advise whether to go for these types of players or avoid them, as every player's specific circumstances are highly variable. Just know that if this is a route you decide to pursue on waivers, you'll be adding a potential volatile fantasy asset.

Tip 58: Approach choosing players off waivers like you would during the draft: based on the qualities you're looking for.

When the reasons for selecting specific free agents were introduced, we discussed one main point: you want players on your team that have the qualities you value for one particular week in a specific position. Figure out what you need for your situation. There's a vast difference between an explosive, play-making running back with upside who averages less than ten touches a game versus a high floor one who you know will get you a solid 15-20 touches each week but may not sneak into the end zone regularly. The beauty about waivers is you decide what you want and how long you want it for; let what you feel you *need* guide you when you're struggling to make a decision.

Tip 59: It will be hard – and you will make many wrong ones throughout the season – but try not to overthink your waiver wire decisions.

This whole section has explored the benefits and strategies surrounding which players to add to your roster, with the small caveat of **making sure the**

added player will be better than the one you are giving up. A risk/reward analysis is vital (like mentioned in *Tip 55*), and you should go with your gut if it's a close decision in the end. But in reality, the decisions are never that easy. I've spent many sleepless nights before the priority deadline hits, thinking, *who should I give up for a waiver player? Which waiver add should I take? Is this player really going to be better than this person I'm getting rid of?*

You will make wrong decisions. You will go back and forth trying to decide who you think will be better. In reality, there's no true way to know until the games are played, which is what makes fantasy football so exciting but also frustrating if you make a couple more wrong decisions than right ones. Do your research, decide if you are ready to move on from a current player, and try your best not to *waiver* (see what I did there? I'm surprised it took me this long to make that joke) with your decision once you have come to one. Hopefully, the fantasy gods will help your decision pay off in the end.

Trades

We just dove into the endless possibilities the waiver wire can provide for your fantasy football team week after week. But what if you are *really* eyeing a player from another fantasy manager's team and wishing you could have them on your roster? Well, good news: trading players is a possibility (and a fun one at that) within fantasy football leagues as well.

I. Risk vs. Reward

Tip 60: Like in the draft and when selecting players off waivers, make sure to do risk/reward analyses as they are vital when making trades.

Did you think figuring out who to draft, and then later on, who to give up, was an important task to weigh outcomes for? If you decide to offer a trade to another team (or someone offers you one), it may be an even more difficult decision. On the one hand, if you are proposing a trade for a fellow league member's second running back, you can't just give him any old player from your bench. You have to give up someone close in value to the person you are asking for. And to make it worth your opponent's time, you'll have to try to make it a player they could really use to improve their team.

Aren't you supposed to be making it *harder* for other fantasy managers to succeed? In the end, you want to have the best team in your league. However, if you need something from someone else, you have to be willing to give them something they want and need as well. You won't be able just to toss your weakest player aside as you do with waivers. It will be a pretty challenging decision to figure out who to 'offer up' for the guy you want, but one that has to be made if you really want a particular player.

Tip 61: Don't feel obligated to take a trade you don't want.

Trading players is an entirely optional but compellingly strategic part of the game. In some leagues, trading happens extremely seldomly; in others, it occurs weekly. It all comes down to the amount of strategy you want to invest in the game.

If you get offered a trade, you may be caught totally off guard if you haven't had any experience with one before. Maybe you look at the offer and think *that's not a bad trade, but I wasn't really looking to give up that player from my team.* This mentality is totally fine. Definitely consider it if it's something reasonable, and you can even put forward a *counter-offer* (reject the specific offer that was given to you but propose something else/something similar) if you like. Still, you have every right to decline it and move on with your season as well, with no harm done.

Tip 62: If multiple players are being traded by at least one of the teams involved, balance the long-term impacts on the depth of your roster.

To make matters even more complicated, picture a situation involving a trade with a greater quantity of players on one side, not just a 'one-for-one' trade. I'll never forget one year when I was offered a wide receiver, ranked in the top-five coming into the season

- right around Week 4. The other manager wanted my second running back *and* one of my starting wide receivers. Part of me was very intrigued to get a top wideout and still have my top running back (he wanted my RB2, remember), something that would have been tough to get in the draft. However, the other side of this argument was that I would be out two key players and would only have a replacement for one. My league mate needed running backs pretty badly as his primary one just had a season-ending injury. He also had a pretty deep receiving core, so he was willing to part with his main one because he had some decent fill-ins.

As enticing as this offer was, I decided to hang with my original team and decline the trade. For a little more background: even though it was my RB2, I selected him in the second round of the draft. I had also chosen the wideout he was targeting in the fourth round. They may not have been in the top five at their position, but they were still up there in overall ratings. Having a balanced team is vital; no one can have an entire team of all-stars, so choosing what to give up to ensure depth is the name of the game.

The reason this trade stuck out to me so much is that barely one week after I declined the trade, that RB2 I was bragging about earlier ended up with an injury that kept him sidelined for eight weeks (aka most of my season). As previously stated throughout this book: no matter how much logic you use, just like in the actual game of football, things out of your control will happen. You have to be ready for anything!

Side Note*: If you receive two players in a trade, but you only give away one, that means you will have to give up another player to waivers for the trade to process. It ensures your roster size remains the same as everyone else's. If you are the one relinquishing two players and only acquiring one back in a trade, you can freely add a free agent from the waiver wire as well to complete your full roster (without having to surrender anyone else).

II. Future Draft Picks

Tip 63: Trading future draft picks is a long-term strategy for the 'tradee,' but if you can't win now as the 'trader,' it won't be worth giving these picks up in the long run.

In standard fantasy leagues that stay together with the same members year after year, rules will sometimes allow for managers to trade for future draft picks (just like in the actual NFL, if you're familiar). For instance: if you are interested in trading for a player on someone else's team, you may feel you just don't have anyone your opponent wants or that you are willing to hand over. One thing you could do, is offer (or add as an additional 'asset') a future draft pick for the upcoming season as part of the deal.

Doing this causes two things to happen: first, the person receiving the draft pick (the *tradee*) will gain a heavy advantage in the following season's draft in whatever round they receive this pick. Second, the team trading away their future draft pick (the *trader* in this situation) has to be truly set on winning *this* year because the following year, they are going to be giving everyone a head start (they will have at least one less pick than everyone else in the corresponding season's draft). If this is a late-round pick, its ramifications aren't as serious. If you are trying to obtain a star player and you start throwing in a second or third-round pick in next year's draft, you're now setting yourself up for an extreme disadvantage in the following season. A word to the wise: only give up a major draft pick if you really have the chance to 'win it all' in the current season. And even then, as with every move you make in fantasy football, realize what you're coughing up for what you're receiving.

Many standard leagues don't do participate in trading future draft picks, though. Sometimes, this can be due to turnover in fantasy managers each year; other times, there is no general interest in anything outside the current season. There may be a variety of reasons that this may not be a part of your league.

Side Note: This tip on future draft pick trading caution is for standard leagues primarily. Trading draft picks in other types of leagues is a common, built-in strategy. While the same cautions need to be taken, these non-standard leagues keep many of the same players year after year, making this strategy more similar to a real-life NFL team. We'll jump more into other types of fantasy leagues in Chapter 5.

III. Vetoing Trades

Tip 64: Don't veto trades, but instead, talk with your commissioner about how they will handle any unfair proposals.

One of the most highly controversial features on many fantasy football platforms is the ability to veto a trade made by league managers. Essentially, after an exchange is agreed upon by the parties involved, a message will trigger from your fantasy platform, telling all of the other fantasy managers the details of the trade. The other league members then have a short period (usually 48 hours) to vote against it if they wish.

The presumable reason for this feature is to stop any 'helping a friend out' situations or one-sided trades that cheat some players that aren't as familiar with the game. Great intentions, but the downside is people can just veto these trades if they are bitter about them. I've seen managers vote against trades because *they* weren't offered an exchange. I've witnessed trade rejections due to a team near the top of the league standings being involved in the trade, so other members deemed the trade 'unfair.' Grudges can even be held when one fantasy manager turned down a trade initially but is now suddenly not ok with someone else carrying out the same offer. These happen *way* more than you would expect when you really get into the weeds of the competition. All it takes is one sore loser or a rough Sunday afternoon, and one-click can anonymously ruin a perfectly fine trade. Think of the trades that happen in the NFL; both parties agree on the transaction, and if not, it doesn't happen. That's the purpose of trades in fantasy football too.

A workaround to ensure teams aren't cheating in any way when trading is to instead have the commissioner evaluate each trade briefly for any sort of misconduct, considering the players and parties involved. It would not allow league members to use the veto feature (the commissioner of your league can easily turn it off). Many people may think, *but that's a dictatorship! Vetoing allows a democracy-type voting system!* And I get it; that is what makes this pretty controversial across the game. But your commissioner has a role in ensuring the league runs smoothly. Trying to override a random angry veto and hear everyone's opinion about a situation that isn't theirs to deal with is much harder than the alternative of using the commissioner's duties for what they are for—worried about the commissioner having the ability to cheat the system by abusing his/her power? Worst case, you can always nominate someone prior to the season commencing to evaluate any trades the commissioner is involved in for complete transparency. The point is, everyone would love a leg up on the competition. Still, helping a friend out doesn't seem very beneficial to the person assisting. Taking light of a situation where someone is hurting a more novice fantasy manager won't do that person any favors either. Expect this to happen less, and rely on your commissioner to do their job (I told you it was like a job!) correctly to ensure everyone has a blast.

Playoffs

Yes, my friends. To find a true winner in every great sport, the best of the best must battle it out in the playoffs. Fantasy football is no different. So, how do these high-stakes games work? How is the true champion crowned at the end of a competitive season? Here are the most common playoff scenarios in standard fantasy football leagues.

I. Playoff Rules

Tip 65: Learn and remember how the playoffs work in your league prior to the start of the season.

It is important to note that the fantasy playoffs don't coincide with the actual NFL playoff weeks. Instead, your fantasy league playoffs will be some variation of the last few weeks of the regular season in the NFL. It is to ensure that all teams take the field during your league playoffs; in the actual NFL postseason, there are obviously a good number of teams who don't make it (aka, your players may not be active). It wouldn't make a ton of sense for fantasy purposes.

The playoffs will run one of two ways in your standard league:

Divisions:

If your league has divisions, the teams with the best win-loss record in each division will automatically go to the playoffs. Any other open spots in the playoffs go to teams with the best records remaining (wild card teams), not taking division into account. To clarify further, let's say six total teams go to the playoffs, and there are four divisions in your 12-team league. The four division winners make the postseason automatically. The remaining two teams are decided by the best remaining records, not related to divisional placement. Even if the top two teams remaining are in the same division, they would proceed to the playoffs. It is pretty identical to the NFL as they also use divisional winners and best remaining records to place their teams.

No Divisions/Head-to-Head (Standard):

You may remember the Head-to-Head scoring type from Chapter 1. It is the most common standard-setting and carries over into the playoffs as well. If your league doesn't have divisions, the teams with the best records are in. If six teams make it to the playoffs in your league, then it will be the winningest six teams in your league.

Side Note: Remember: if your league uses a Points Only scoring type for the season, there are generally no playoffs. There aren't head-to-head matchups during the season, and instead, your points are totaled for your individual team each week. The team with the most points at the end of the season wins your league, so no playoffs are necessary.

Tip 66: Be mindful of your tie-breaker rules for season standings, especially late in the year.

What if you run into an instance where three teams are tied for the last remaining spot in the playoffs? Who would advance? Often leagues will give the advantage to a team that has more total points scored throughout the entire season, pending a tie. It normally breaks a tie pretty quickly as points can be broken down to the tenths or hundredths decimal place quite often. However, in the small chance there still is a tie, or if your league decides to forgo the total season points scored tie-breaker option, sometimes head-to-head records are used, like in the actual NFL (and also division records, if the league uses divisions). There are a few other tie-breakers in place due to the small chance a tie still exists, but these are the first two (and deciding two) in the majority of cases.

II. Playoff Seeding and Reseeding

Playoff games have the same scoring and rules as any other regular season fantasy game. What's different is how your opponent in the following week's matchup is determined (if you are lucky enough to advance to the next round).

Let's use a six-team playoff example for this explanation. Each team will be ranked (first is the best, sixth is the worst in this case) and the best teams in each round generally get to play the worst teams in each round. To start off the first round of the playoffs, there will usually be a bye week in this situation (a first-round bye to the top two teams) because of the odd number of teams that would be remaining if all six teams play this round. Think about it: if six teams play each other in the first round, there would only be three left in the second round. It is why a bye is given to the top two teams, allowing them to automatically advance to the second round of the postseason without playing in the first one.

Continuing with this scenario: the third seed would play the sixth, and the fourth seed would play the fifth, while the first and second seeds automatically advance to the second round of the playoffs with their byes. In the second round, what is known as **reseeding** will typically occur. The first seeded team will play the lowest-seeded team remaining, and the second-seeded team will play the highest-seeded one left. And the final round of the postseason will match up as the last two teams left standing for the ultimate championship.

Now, in saying this, this particular example shows the *typical* way playoffs are run. As we talked about in the first few chapters, every league can have a different setup. Some leagues may have only four teams advance to the playoffs, or some may have eight; in both of these instances, bye weeks wouldn't be necessary.

Tip 67: Heavily push for a playoff scenario that reseeds teams to ensure the fairest play.

The exception to all of this information about seeding is when leagues don't actually reseed once the playoffs are underway. Teams are always ranked going into the postseason, but there is a setting (which I highly *don't* recommend using) that doesn't change the seeding as the playoffs progress past the first round. No reseeding means the first-place team wouldn't necessarily play the worst remaining seed left, which it (well-deservingly) earned the right to play.

After all of these rules and efforts have been put into place throughout the season, it could come crashing to an abrupt end without a simple reseeding rule in place. This method of organizing matchups during the playoffs is used in the majority of professional sports' playoffs. It guarantees fairness and pays tribute to a team's success accomplished during the season.

III. Playoff Formats

After determining the rules of which teams move forward to the playoffs in your league and which opponent each team will match up against as they progress, it is also vital to know the *type* of playoff format you are participating in. There are essentially two main setups that standard leagues typically choose from:

Single Elimination Playoffs:

In this type of playoff format, it's a 'one-and-done' system. No matter the round, if you lose to another team in a playoff game, you are eliminated. If you beat an opposing team, you advance to the next round. In one single game, whoever has the most points in a head-to-head matchup, moves on.

Two-Week Combined Playoffs:

The two-week combined playoff format introduces a 'series' structure. Other sports such as baseball, basketball, or hockey incorporate a series of postseason games. They play multiple times in a row against the same opponent, and the winner of the majority of matchups advances to the next round. In this structure of fantasy football play, the same two opponents will play each other *two weeks* in a row, and whichever team has the most combined points at the end of the two weeks prevails.

So, if your playoffs start in Week 14, you'll set a lineup like usual for that week, as will your opponent. Even if your opponent 'beats' you that week, it won't matter. Why? Because you play them again in Week 15 (you are able to change your lineup in this next game as well), and your total scored points from both weeks are what will determine your fate against your opponent. This sort of playoff format is most commonly seen when only four teams advance to the playoffs. Primarily because for two weeks of the playoffs, there will be the same four teams facing off against each other. This will then be followed by another two weeks for the championship. That's already a four-week postseason, making it tough to go any longer, which would be the case if any more teams were added.

Side Note: Either playoff style (divisions or no divisions/head-to-head) can play with either of these formats.

Tip 68: Have your championship scheduled to finish the week BEFORE the real NFL regular season ends.

What week of the NFL regular season should your fantasy playoffs start and end? Most leagues have three of four weeks' worth of them, so why not just start the week that will allow you to end on the final week of the regular season?

Imagine some of the best teams in the NFL in the last week of the regular season. Maybe a team already clinched their entire division, a first-round bye, home-field advantage even, and they aren't able to really move around in the standings much before the last week of play. What do you often see coaches do in this situation? You guessed it: bench their star players. Now imagine your impressive fantasy quarterback and wide receiver are also on that incredible football team that's already clinched first place, and the coach decided to give them a break to rest up for the NFL postseason. How is that going to affect your fantasy team? Wouldn't that be the ultimate letdown? If your starting players were _benched_ for the most critical game of the entire year?! Think about it; if you are still alive in the playoffs in this specific scenario (your fantasy league has games being played up until the last week of the NFL regular season), that would be your championship!

Many leagues opt to end the fantasy season the week *before* the last regular season NFL game to keep the playing field as fair as possible for the two teams left standing in their championship. I've had my share of leagues where this wasn't the case, though. I was up by 70 points after the first week in a two-week combined points championship and ended up losing by just two points when the final score was tallied between the two weeks. Both my star running back *and* wide receiver (my top two draft picks on the year) were resting for that last game due to their respective team situations going into the NFL playoffs. If you are unlucky enough to be in this type of scenario but lucky enough to have made it to the championship, do what you can to prepare, if possible, and demand your commissioner change it for next season!

IV. Additional Playoff Tips

Tip 69: Don't overthink a playoff round. Continue to do the things that got you to this point.

Well, you made it to your league's fantasy playoffs; congrats! Your mind is probably racing with ideas of how to play even *better* now that your season is on the line. In reality, though, there's a reason you got to this spot. You were able to put together a squad week after week during your season that outplayed enough of your fellow fantasy managers to put you in a top position in your league. The best advice here is to try not to overthink the playoffs too much. You will feel the need to treat these games with a little bit more nervous energy when making your decisions, but just like many professional athletes say, it's just another game. Continue to do the things you did well all year, and let your strategy prevail.

Tip 70: Take even bigger risks on the waiver wire, though, as it's ride or die when you get to playoff time.

The one exception to the rule of *continue to play 'your' game* that I just harped on in *Tip 69* may come when the waiver wire is taken into consideration. If you make any moves at this point (which you absolutely still can, but maybe won't feel the need to unless there is a gaping hole due to an injury), the difference now is you don't have to worry about the future, too much.

I bet plenty of times during the season; you'll debate on a decision to claim a player based on their longevity on your team and not just on the one upcoming week. In the playoffs, you won't have to think about that as much. Sure, there could be multiple weeks you have to account for, but that number is finite. It could help you weigh the risks and rewards slightly more effectively. There's also the mentality of you absolutely could be around for only one more week, so you have to make things happen right now. Whatever way you choose to think about this, taking bigger 'risks' on the waiver wire shouldn't upend your season-long strategy but instead help solidify a chance to ensure those bragging rights in a short time.

Tip 71: I know it stinks, but set a lineup in your consolation bracket.

What if you don't happen to be one of the lucky ones to finish with a good enough season to make it to the postseason? Unfortunately, that is a widespread occurrence. You may have the *oh well, see you next year* mentality, but 'lucky' for you, there is generally still a little bit more fantasy football to play. Most fantasy platforms have what's called a consolation bracket, which is basically a nice way to say 'games for the losers to battle it out for the remaining rankings.'

People may often ignore their team once they become disqualified from the playoffs (you are *also* in a consolation bracket if you make it to the playoffs but get eliminated before the championship). But all of these games are played to determine the overall standings for the entire season for your league. There are a few reasons to play these games, though, as meaningless as they may sound to you.

First, it stinks getting the last place. Plus, if your league happens to have a league 'punishment' as we talked about in Chapter 1, you will want to fight not to be the worst-ranked team. So play the season out until the end.

Second, there are no advantages to losing to get a lower final standing (e.g., to get a higher draft pick) in most standard leagues. The upcoming season's draft isn't decided by previous season standings – like it is in the NFL - the majority of the time. The draft order is randomly determined mere minutes before the draft begins as a standard across most platforms, even if you're participating in a straight draft type.

Third, you get another week (or more) of fantasy football; take advantage of it before a long, boring offseason where only distant dreams of returning to your new favorite hobby will exist.

League Tips for Enjoyable In-Season Play

Tip 72: Watch games with your fellow fantasy managers, especially those you are playing head-to-head against in a given week.

Undoubtedly, sports are more exciting to watch with others who enjoy them as well. When it comes to fantasy football, there is a whole different level of entertainment that comes with watching football games on television. And who better to watch these battles with than your opponents! While it may not be possible every week and may be particularly hard if you don't live geographically close to one another, do what you can to experience some of the games with at least a few of your league mates throughout the season. Not only should the trash talk be epic, but it brings another definition to the word 'competition' when you can watch your squad (hopefully) crush your fellow fantasy manager's team across a table full of snacks.

Tip 73: Have some sort of messaging system for your league.

Whether it's a simple group text, an expansive league message board, making use of the chat feature on your fantasy football platform, or another group communication application, set up a system so you can feel like you are part of your own personal fantasy football community. Not everyone in your league will get together for all of the games, but they will be hyper-focusing on their scores each week. Smack talk, game highlights, or just general NFL gossip; have a place where you can communicate all of your football thoughts and build camaraderie with your league.

Tip 74: Fantasy football is an emotional game; take that into account when playing.

The draft, a trade, waivers, or a ruling on who to start in a particular week; all strategic decisions can get caught up in emotions as well. What if there are three wide receivers you were eyeing in the draft, but one from your favorite team is right behind them in ADP? Should you pass on him? Your friend offers you a trade that you feel will help your team, but it would require giving up a player that you actually got an autograph from at a game the season prior. Do you go through with the trade? Maybe you just 'have a feeling' a guy from your bench is going to do better this week, but logic defies those thoughts. Is ignoring the strategic plan that got you the team you have today a smart move?

Fantasy football is a game. Part of every game is competing and winning and how you feel about how you do these two things. It would be a mistake to make every critical decision based on emotions alone, but some of the best professional athletes, CEOs, movie stars, etc., got where they are today based on following their hearts. Let your emotions guide you when coming to conclusions with different parts of fantasy football, but just be sure to use them wisely. Enjoy every bit of this experience that you can. If that means choosing a running back off waivers that you like better over another one with a similar value that you don't like as much, knock yourself out. Just be sure to balance emotional and strategic decision-making throughout the entirety of the season.

Tip 75: Have some friendly outside wagers based on your fantasy results.

There will be plenty of times where you make a bold move in fantasy football, and you don't feel like it was appreciated enough by others. Or you are playing a good friend in an upcoming week, and you are giddy over the idea of crushing him/her with the leadership of your top free agent find. In Chapter 1, we talked about having a 'buy-in' for the league to ensure people are taking the game seriously, winners are being rewarded, and the majority of the managers lose more than just their season's hopes and dreams at the end of each league year. Why not add a little extra enticement for intra-season play?

What if you bet your friend the next round of appetizers if your new waiver wire adds scores over 20 points that week? Maybe you finally accept that trade you've been on the fence about from a fellow league member if his running back gets two or more touchdowns this week. Small, side prop bets can add to the fun of your weekly competition. Don't go crazy with any extreme bets that could deteriorate the core of your team's well-being (or your financial one, for that matter). Still, frequently people enjoy having a chance to flaunt some fun statistical 'knowledge,' as it can add some fun to the overall experience.

Tip 76: Again, don't cheat.

This was discussed during the trade-vetoing section, but honestly, cheating in fantasy football is just not a smart move. If you found a loophole in the league settings that helps at all, it probably won't for too long. If you do wrong to another participant of your league, karma is bound to bite you way quicker than you expect. Just like in any game, don't take the fun out of this amazing competition for a quick fix. Just don't do it.

Chapter 4 Review

In this chapter, you will learn about the following topics:

- Different waiver wire types that can be used in your league
- Particular options and reasons to target players on the waiver wire throughout the season
- Successful trade techniques and how to best assess their value
- Specific playoff rules and format types for your fantasy football league
- Unique approaches to enjoy your fantasy football season for its entire duration

Chapter 5: Which League Type is Best for You?

Throughout the past four chapters of this book, you have been pummeled with numerous rules, tips, and strategies to navigate your way through *standard* fantasy leagues. While there can be quite a few rule variations for these standard leagues (which we will discuss in this chapter), the basics for any standard, season-long fantasy football league are similar. Position and point options can apply pretty regularly (with few exceptions) across the board. However, did you know that there is an assortment of additional league types out there as well? Some of them can last for the duration of only one single game, and others continue for years.

Tip 77: Try your hand at different versions of fantasy football as you deem fit for your interests.

What you have become familiar with (the 'standard' fantasy football league) is commonly referred to amongst the fantasy football community as a **season-long or redraft** league. These names are given because you make decisions relating to an entire season worth of games with your same players, but the following season, you draft an entirely different team. This chapter will highlight these other types of fantasy options, along with some specialized rules to make standard leagues completely different from what you have become accustomed to. We'll even talk about a fantasy football playoff game that follows teams in the actual NFL postseason (quite unlike the standard leagues we discussed). Buckle up because your mind is about to be blown with these alternative options to play your favorite sports stats game.

Specialized Rule Changes in Standard Leagues

As I alluded to on several occasions, there are many variations on standard league play. Sometimes it could be just a small rule change that makes these leagues break away from the norm (such as an added bonus statistic as discussed in *Tip 13*); other times, it can be a larger modification in play. Adding different positions or changing how the scores are calculated for specific positions are all possibilities with unique customization.

I. Quarterback Scoring Change Leagues

Remember how in Chapter 1, we discussed how you only need one quarterback for your starting lineup, and they get fewer points to 'even the playing field' with the rest of the positions? Well, forget that logic here. The first few rule changes we'll discuss will revolve around the quarterback position. What if your league wants to make the quarterback position's point potential larger instead of consistent with the rest of the league? Kind of like it is in the real-life game?

Tip 78: If you want to make the quarterback position have a slight edge and more closely relate to their actual NFL value, try a point adjustment to increase it.

Many different revisions can be made to a quarterback's scoring uptake. What about allowing their passing touchdowns to be worth six points? That will undoubtedly bring the value of the quarterback closer to the top of the list. What if they also deducted three or four points for turning the ball over instead of their original one or two? The conversation potentially gets more interesting if you are looking at a quarterback who isn't as protective of the ball as they should be. All in all, the quarterback position is one of the most admired ones in all of the sports. Any added risk, rewards, or special circumstances to make this position even more unique can bring some extra entertainment to your league.

II. Two-Quarterback Leagues

This position alteration is pretty straightforward. In this instance, you'll need two quarterbacks on your starting roster.

Quarterbacks may be jumping higher on your draft list now, seeing that – in a 12-team league, for example – 24 quarterbacks (out of the 32 starters available in any given week) will need to be in starting lineups the entire year. And we all know the 20th ranked quarterback isn't coming close compared to the 5th rated one.

III. Superflex Leagues

Another fun positional tweak is to have your flex position turned into a **Superflex** one (or, in typical cases, have one regular flex *and* another Superflex spot in your starting lineup). Superflex essentially 'super charges' your flex position. Usually, remember, you can have a running back, wide receiver, or tight end in your FLEX. In Superflex leagues, you can also have a *quarterback* as an option in this spot, allowing for more roster flexibility.

Like with the two-quarterback leagues, you have a decision to make when drafting -and throughout the year - to ensure this spot on your roster performs well. While this is a dream situation for managers that love difficult decisions, it's a quite different scenario for the leagues with a two-quarterback requirement. The Superflex situation is an optional quarterback insertion on a weekly basis, whereas the two-quarterback leagues require you have two starting every week. And you thought your regular flex decisions were tough to make...

Tip 79: In two-quarterback, Superflex, or quarterback point adjustment leagues, a quarterback's value will increase substantially, so change your draft strategy and in-season management accordingly.

These three scenarios open up an entirely new can of worms when draft strategy and in-season management are considered. You don't have to put a quarterback in the Superflex necessarily, but they sure do seem to rack up many points. But will a lower-tier signal-caller perform better (on average) than a third running back or wide receiver at that spot? And outside of that, does that mean quarterbacks will fly off the draft board faster since many will be choosing two? In two-quarterback leagues, you know you'll have to make this play since you are required two on your starting roster, but how soon should you draft them? And what do you do if one gets injured or has a bye week? In leagues where quarterbacks are accumulating more points, their value definitely skyrockets as well, but do you make your selections differently because of this?

IV. Tight End Premium Leagues

While the tight end position is a familiar one, it's continuously one of the more difficult ones to succeed with in the fantasy arena. As discussed in Chapter 3, there are very few top-tier tight ends each season; and after those few, the drop-off is substantial. We're talking to the extent that a good deal of fantasy managers end up just scanning the waiver wire each week and throwing up a matchup prayer (hoping they can find a tight end on waivers that has an easy matchup against an opposing defense). Maybe you get lucky and find a tight end who sees a few targets and possibly falls into the end zone, but it's tough to see that consistently out of most tight ends. In the tight end, premium leagues, that all changes.

Tip 80: Provided you want to balance the playing field with tight ends and their counterparts (wide receivers and running backs), tight end premium leagues can really make for a thrilling experience.

Instead of having the interest level at the tight end position dwindle throughout the season if you don't walk away with one of the top few studs, their value now explodes because of one simple modification: more points per reception. Generally, tight end premium leagues give these players 1.5 points per reception (whereas everyone else is either getting 0.5 or 1 in these circumstances). It's also not uncommon to see 1 PPR for leagues that give other pass catchers 0.5 PPR. Overall, though, 1.5 PPR tends to give the position that extra boost in scoring to truly match their overall values up with other pass-catching options on your roster.

III. Individual Defensive Player (IDP) Leagues

Tip 81: Give an IDP league a shot if you have a particular interest in defenders or if you want an added research component to the game.

Individual Defensive Player (or IDP) leagues are the one specialized league variation that actually adds positions that we haven't addressed before. These roster spots are added to separate the team defenses from the individual defenders themselves. Some leagues may just have one 'general' defender position, which allows you to draft any defensive player for this slot. Others may have spots for specific positions: defensive back, defensive lineman, or linebacker. The scoring here is variable as well, depending on the emphasis leagues want to place on particular defender statistics. A good example of what you may see points granted for are tackles (0.5 or 1), sacks and forced turnovers (2 or 3), and touchdowns (the usual 6). Points for pass deflections, tackles for losses, and even tackle assists (when you share a tackle with someone) can be awarded as well.

Tip 82: Big name defenders are NOT always the best players to have on your roster in IDP leagues; it can be beneficial to target ones who tend to accumulate a wealth of tackles each game instead.

What if you're thinking I don't know a lot of defenders? Well, that's ok. It's actually not necessarily the best move to just pick a big-name defender to have in your IDP spot(s). Maybe there is a great defensive end that brings in ten-plus sacks every season but spread out over the course of the entire year, is that enough? What if they also only average around 30 or 40 tackles a season? Even though tackles will provide you fewer points, chances are there will be some linebackers out there (and even some defensive backs, potentially) that can get you upwards of 100 of them if you're lucky.

Use historical statistics (their average tackle amounts in previous seasons) to help you see which players make the most plays happen on the field. It is almost like finding a receiver that is targeted frequently instead of one that scores double-digit touchdowns on very few catches (like in Tip 28). Remember: it's all about the volume. In this instance, it's about the volume of plays a specific defender can make versus a few huge plays. Also, don't be scared to toss a defender aside in any given week and replace them with a better available option. These types of players (like kickers and team defense/special teams) are overlooked quite a bit; make sure you aim to have ones on your team that will give you a consistent number of points to add to your total score each week.

VI. Keeper Leagues

Some leagues keep entire rosters year after year; we'll talk about those in the following section. But what if you're not ready for that kind of commitment? Just like a long-term relationship, you have to really work at that type of league and be in it for the long haul. An excellent step up from standard season-long leagues – but not the whole two-story house and white picket fence scenario – are keeper leagues.

Tip 83: For added long-term strategy in your standard, season-long league, give keepers a try.

In keeper leagues, you literally keep a specific number of players for the following season on your roster. There are various options on how many keepers you can retain each year, how many seasons in a row you can keep them for, and what you have to sacrifice to hold onto them. You didn't think you could just stick with your top three studs at no cost, did you?

One of the first leagues I was a part of decided to give keepers a try after a few seasons of standard redraft play. At first, we began with keeping up to three players, and after you decided who those players were, you couldn't keep them again the season after. Also, we had to give up a draft pick in the upcoming season's draft; it was the draft pick before the round you drafted your keeper in. Let me explain: for an upcoming season, I decided to keep the running back I selected in the fourth round of the draft the season prior. The only way I could do that was to give up my third-round pick in the season I was keeping that player in (I drafted him in the fourth round the year prior, had to give up my third-round selection for the current drafting year).

It adds some strategy to decide if that player is worth keeping since you have to give up a higher pick than he was valued at a year ago. Sometimes that pays off; if he was a top-five running back, he is absolutely worth losing a third-round pick for if he has a high chance of having a repeat season. Other times it's not worth keeping the player, like if you feel he'll perform at about the same level he was drafted (have the same ADP again). Another interesting thing to note is in my particular experience, this was set up, so you weren't able to keep anyone you selected in the first round since there is no higher round (than the first round) draft pick to give up in the upcoming draft. Over the years, that morphed back and forth to only being able to keep up to two players and to have to give up two draft picks above where the player was selected the previous year (to keep a fourth-rounder, I'd have to give up my second-round pick in the current drafting year). It was fun to experiment with and weigh the possible outcomes of keeping some consistency on your fantasy squad as the seasons continued.

Side Note: Keepers only really make sense to do if you have the same league members playing each year. There are ways to figure out a fair way to have a new fantasy manager come in to take over an existing team and decide who to keep – or just make that one team start from scratch with no keepers – but you can see how that may cause some 'fairness' issues in the grand scheme of things.

Besides these six more common spins on standard league positions and scoring, there are literally hundreds of other things you can do to customize your league further. Want to increase the impact of team defense/special teams? Start them off with 15 points instead of the standard 5 or 10. Tired of kickers? Nix them from your league's lineups. Want to have three starting receivers or four FLEX spots in your league's starting roster? Why not? I've personally been in a league that gave you points for each first down a player got. I had no idea how to plan for the draft in that situation; I just hoped they moved the yardsticks often!

You may join a league with some of these specialized rules or a wacky assortment of others; either way, they are implemented to add to the fun, excitement, and value for a range of different players, so buckle up and select your team accordingly! Also, for some of the other league types that are about to be discussed, these unique rules can apply. Oftentimes, these rules can be more the 'norm' in certain situations. While I would need a separate book to give all of the details on each of these, here is a brief introduction to various fantasy football competition types you can participate in.

Dynasty Leagues

Tip 84: While you don't necessarily want to start your fantasy football journey in a dynasty league, you should give one a try if you end up loving the game.

Dynasty leagues: for the ultimate fantasy footballers. This variety of fantasy football not only combines your knowledge and love for the game (and statistics) of football, but this type of league allows you to run a team like an actual NFL franchise owner, in charge of every step along the way. In your dynasty league's inauguration season, your team is drafted, and you continue to have those players on your team year after year (unless they retire or you cut/trade them). Talk about your long-term commitment. This style of fantasy play isn't for the casual fan, but if you love the game and want to invest more time and leave a deeper imprint on it, a dynasty league can be one of the greatest experiences in fantasy football.

I. Rules

The rules in dynasty formats are based on the ones from season-long leagues. Some variation of the same positions, scoring, and league settings are used, but most likely with many added twists like we talked about in the previous _'Specialized Rule Changes in Standard Leagues'_ section. It tends to keep things interesting each successive year.

A fair amount of these scoring rules/positional differences (specifically, tight end premium and Superflex rules) are not even considered 'unique' in dynasty leagues. Instead, they are more a regularity to truly ensure league members take numerous strategies into account for long-term success.

One stark contrast in these leagues is that they tend to have *much* larger bench sizes; some can get up to 17 players riding the sidelines. The reason: to make sure from the onset of the draft that you have an array of options to pull from as this is your team for the long haul. The waiver wire still exists but focuses more on new trending players than ones that you didn't have room for on your initial team. This assumption allows the 'worthwhile' players to be rostered before the beginning of the season – just like in the NFL. Don't worry; just because waivers aren't as enticing as they are in redraft leagues, *trades* become a much more important asset that creates an entirely enthralling (and NFL-like) fantasy experience in dynasty leagues. More on that shortly.

There can even be *additional* positions outside of all of your starters and bench players – known as **taxi squad players** - which basically replicate practice squad players in the NFL. Similar to the IR spots briefly mentioned at the beginning of Chapter 1, they don't take up space on your roster, but you shield them from other fantasy managers claiming them. You can bring them up to your active roster pending you release a different player. It is commonplace to hideaway rookies drafted lower in drafts as many of them (outside of the top performers) tend to take a few seasons to build up efficient playing time.

II. Drafting

In dynasty leagues, the initial startup draft to your
league has *very* high stakes. To start, some people do
one combined draft, where all available players –
rookies and others – are selected just like in a
standard redraft league (except you are obviously not
going to be redrafting). Others may start up their
dynasty leagues by doing one draft with all of the
players available in the current NFL landscape except
the rookies, followed by a separate one with *only* the
rookies.

The former is a complete option that allows fantasy
managers to assess all players equally. Still, the latter
can relate closely to an actual NFL franchise entering
the league (where they add current NFL players to
their roster and participate in selecting players out of
college in the NFL Draft). Snake drafts can have the
same benefits that are seen in redraft, season-long
leagues. Still, in initial startup dynasty league drafts,
auction-style drafting can create an intriguing
atmosphere of controlling a franchise. As mentioned
in *Tip 18*, these are much lengthier but have many
upsides in leagues with a great deal of dedication, like
these.

Tip 85: Assessing your team's future needs will be crucial in achieving success in consecutive rookie drafts each offseason.

What happens after the ever-so-crucial *first* draft of
your dynasty league? With the depth each fantasy

manager has, along with the fact that they will be keeping their entire team for the foreseeable future, are there any more drafts? There are, actually. There is a draft each impending season, but with *rookies only*.

Some players retire, some underperform; this doesn't mean you're stuck with them (or scrambling for anything you can find on waivers) for eternity. Dynasty leagues are intended to resemble true NFL general team management structure closely. And with that comes a GM's favorite offseason activity: the college draft. Each draft your league holds before the upcoming season will be composed of all the rookies coming into the NFL. Fantasy managers will be able to assess their needs and continue building the future of their dynasty, just like in the real game. These drafts are usually performed in a straight draft format as this correlates with the NFL college drafting style, attempting to achieve long-term competitive fairness across the league (see the *'Straight Drafts'* section for a refresher on these draft types).

III. Strategy

Tip 86: Pay special attention to the age of a player you select to be a member of your dynasty team.

One indispensable quality an athlete needs to have to play successfully for countless years is youth. Of course, it's great to have a veteran 37-year-old quarterback in a redraft league, but is it in dynasty? For a year or two more, they may be great, but if you were a real NFL team, are you starting up a franchise around a team leader with one foot on the way out the door towards retirement? Chances are you'd rather have the 25-year-old who has been lighting up defenses the past few years, as he may potentially be continuing that pattern for the next decade (or more). Age is an added (and major) factor in dynasty leagues. Although, younger players obviously come with some added risk regarding long-term quality play since many of these players haven't been around long enough to prove their longevity. It all adds to the 'general manager' feel of dynasty leagues in that you are constantly making moves not just for the future of the current season but for many years to come to ensure continued success from your franchise.

More specifically, think about the position you are selecting when considering age. A person who can have a big impact on your team for longer will have a higher value in a dynasty league, but that doesn't mean you shouldn't get some veterans to help lead your team either. Balance is key here, and positional effects are as well. For example, the duration of a running back's career is *much* shorter than that of a quarterback. Finding a six-year veteran running back may be a nice short-lived pick, but it may be tough to replenish this vital position in only a few short years. A quarterback in that same situation could be set for another decade of performing, though. Still, there is obviously more to every particular situation than just what's apparent on the outside.

Tip 87: Trade, trade, trade. Without trading, your success in a dynasty will take a hit.

When discussing trading in standard, redraft leagues, we talked about how some people like to implement them, and others have enough going on in the season that they primarily focus their attention on waivers. Dynasty is a different story; without trading in these formats, you are almost bound to flop down the road.

NFL teams make trades all the time. In-season, offseason; teams are continuously assessing their current and future situations. Looking ahead without compromising what's best for the season you are currently in is the utmost vital skill when managing a dynasty team. Trading players and future draft picks can happen even more than waiver wire pickups (due to the increased bench sizes), as they do in the NFL, to secure prolonged success as a franchise.

Tip 88: Dynasty fantasy leagues are multi-year commitments with various rules enforced to ensure your loyalty. Come prepared to be caring for your team throughout the season and all off-season long, and understand that your choices impact your entire league.

After you draft your team, you enjoy a great (or sadly, not-so-great) first season. Guess what? It's not over! If you were to turn on ESPN in the offseason, you tend to see free agent signings, draft analysis, and player projections all year-round. And during these crucial offseason periods, general managers of NFL teams are making moves to brighten the future of their teams. That's what you have to do to ensure your squad is up and running for the following season(s) as well. Always be on top of the latest news and looking for ways to make your dynasty the epitome of achievement in your league.

Dynasty commissioners may even instill rules for in-season plays to have teams not 'tank' (lose games purposely) for a better draft pick as ensuing seasons' rookie drafts are a huge part of long-term dynasty strategy. There may also be penalties enforced to make sure managers don't forget to set their lineups in a given week as well. Because, particularly in dynasty leagues, seemingly small actions by one team can have a major effect on an entire league's present *and* future predicaments.

Way back at *Tip 7*, we discussed friendly wagers to keep the season interesting. Money is always a great enticer for people to keep trying their best. Oftentimes dues are paid to be in dynasty leagues to ensure active participation. However, these contributions can mostly go towards a payout at the end of the season for the winners (although some platforms require payment for participation in dynasty leagues).

Understanding the strategic (and financial) impacts certain moves (or lack thereof) can have on a team can have serious fantasy players deeply contemplating their choices as it will affect their livelihood for many future years. As long as rules are being abided by, all strategies are fair game; just understand they have effects past your current situation.

Daily Fantasy Sports (Football) or DFS

What is the opposite of playing with the same fantasy football team every year? How about having a different one potentially every *game*? **Daily Fantasy Sports or DFS** is a popular fantasy football game that allows you to do just that.

I. Types of DFS Games

The logistics of DFS put a fun spin on the rules we are accustomed to seeing in most fantasy football leagues. While the scoring is similar to standard leagues, the rules and position selections are quite unique.

First, when you select players for your team, you are choosing them for a specific game or a specific set of games for just one NFL week. For a set of games, this can entail all of the collective games on Sunday and Monday combined, just the early Sunday games, or even just the late ones. Another option is to select and play a fantasy game revolving around just *one* of the NFL games on the slate for the week. Whether it's the Sunday evening game or strictly one of the Sunday early afternoon games, the players you choose will all be from one NFL matchup for that specific week. Lastly, there is even the option to play a fantasy 'half' or 'quarter' of a game. In this instance, you select a fantasy team to calculate points from a single game but *only* from the second half or the fourth quarter.

Tip 89: All of these DFS types have their own styles of fun; try a variety of them to see where your niche lies.

Being able to pick a roster for solely a weekend may make you feel invincible and seem like loads of fun. Or maybe you are watching the Monday night game and thinking, *wouldn't it be fun just to have an entire fantasy roster for this game*? Think about how the satisfaction you could get from watching a game where all of your fantasy players were competing? All of this is possible in the DFS style of play, and it's quite an eccentric way to expand the game of fantasy football even further.

II. Choosing Players

Choosing the players to be on your team isn't as simple as it seems, though. You aren't just able to go out and draft the ultimate, all-star fantasy team. Actually, you are given an imaginary budget that you have to split between the players to complete your lineup. Each player will have an allotted 'cost' to their name, with the high performers priced at a much higher rate.

Lineup choices will vary depending on the DFS option you choose. Many of the combined weekend games (multiple games from the weekend in one DFS matchup) will have standard positions, including defenses, although typically not kickers. In a single game, second half only, or fourth quarter only options, you can pick pretty much *any* players you want (depending on the platform you play on), but only a handful of total roster spots to do this with (typically five or six). In the five-player example, you could pick the quarterbacks from both teams and three wide receivers if you wanted to, as long as you stay under the salary cap (your budget). The other twist to these single-game/second-half/fourth-quarter matchups is that they tend to have an 'MVP' spot on the roster. Whichever player you put in this spot will have a multiplier associated with their score, awarding you 1.5 times their points to go towards your final allotment. Pretty cool, huh?

Tip 90: Stacking a quarterback and wide receiver from the same team is a great way to get double the points in DFS games.

How do you decide who to pick with all of these options? A great deal of your decision-making is going to come down to how much money you have in your budget. If you want a really expensive star, how do you build the rest of your team? Should you shoot for depth at *every* position in DFS, as you do in standard leagues? We'll dive into these questions when we further separate the types of games in the next section.

Nonetheless, one popular DFS strategy that can be useful in any situation is called a **stack**. It entails selecting a quarterback and a wide receiver (or tight end sometimes) from the same NFL team as part of your lineup. Think about it: if a quarterback throws a touchdown to their own wide receiver, you'll get points for double the touchdowns and yards! In standard, season-long leagues, this may not be as common due to the full reliance on one team for an entire year; but in a daily matchup, the overall risk is much higher in general when you are picking players, so why not double your odds the gamble pays off? Let's assess that type of risk by discussing the two main matchup styles you can participate in on most daily fantasy platforms.

III. Cash Games vs. Tournaments (or GPPs)

On most platforms, to participate in daily sports (with the most common ones being DraftKings and FanDuel), an entry fee is required. If you're not a bettor, though, that's totally fine. They have buy-ins for as little as ten cents across most of these platforms (and various free entry opportunities as well), essentially protecting your mortgage payments even if you decide to go a little crazy with the number of games you take part in.

There are two basic types of DFS contests that both rely on different strategies for selecting players:

Cash Games:

Cash games are known in daily fantasy sports as the 'safer' bet due to their 50/50 odds of increasing your earnings. These contests typically have small groups of people (some are head-to-head against one other opponent, others can get up to 100 different people), but the winnings will be split evenly amongst the top 50%. The goal with these types of content is to have a *good enough* team to place in the top half of the contest. Since it doesn't 'pay' more to place first or forty-first in a cash game with 100 participants, taking significant risks is not a smart strategy in claiming a piece of these payouts.

___Tip 91: In cash games, don't blow most of your allotted salary on a few top players; balance your lineup and spend your money wisely in these contests.___

Remember - each player will have a different worth, and you have to deduct that worth from your 'salary' to add them to your roster. It can obviously seem limitless when making your first selection. But if you pick a few other people and are suddenly running extremely low on money, your team's depth won't be there. Wisely spending your 'money' is key to having a well-balanced roster in cash games. There are a few types of these contents, all with the same 50/50 odds. Explore these different low-stakes DFS games to find your niche.

Tournaments or Guaranteed Prize Pools (GPPs):

Many DFS participants want to ignore this rule of thinking and go big with a few players and small with the others. This frame of mind is more useful in

tournaments (also known as **Guaranteed Prize Pools or GPPs**), where you find higher payouts for the top-seeded winners.

These exciting contests are your definition of a high-risk/high-reward matchup, though. Who wouldn't want a chance to walk away with potentially *thousands* of dollars from one small entry fee? It may sound nice, but tournaments tend to have a very large quantity of participants (could be in the hundreds of thousands), and only around the top 20% will walk away with any earnings at all; and those winnings will be tiered, giving more to the better set lineups.

Let's presume there is a small, one-dollar buy-in for a tournament with thirty thousand dollars in total prizes. If the top 20% out of, say, 50,000 lineups earn a payout, 10,000 participants will get some form of a prize. Sounds impressive, but this is where the 'tiered' winnings come into play. Out of those 10,000 winners, the bottom 5,000 may only receive $1.50 in total prizes – grossing just fifty cents for making it this far. The tiers only get smaller as they move up, potentially awarding the first-place winner with barely over a grand in winnings (and the second-place person possibly taking home just half of that).

What's important to note here is that the only way to have a chance at a big prize is to take risks in these tournament games. Balance is always good, but if you are trying to score as many points as possible in a single weekend, you may have to pick some outside-the-box players. Possibly a 'sleeper' wide receiver or a low-cost quarterback, so you can collect a nice pair of running back studs to set your lineup apart. In these games, you don't just have to cross the fiftieth percentile hurdle; here, you are maximizing your roster to get the *most total points* to place as high as possible. What are some other ways you can increase your chances in these contests?

Tip 92: While entering into a tournament, submit more than one lineup to the same contest to increase your odds of placing.

You can set one lineup in most cash games, and you hope you place in the top half of the contest. In GPPs, a great way to help your chances of finishing with winnings is by entering *multiple* lineups in the same contest. There are usually limits on how many you can enter into the same tournament, but you can see how your chances can improve this way. Yes, you'll have to dish out more cash, but at least you have a greater chance at the 'lottery winnings' now (almost like buying more than one lottery ticket). Another strategy along these lines is entering the *exact same* lineup for all of your entries, therefore aligning your odds to be all the same. Some people go that route; others like to make different lineups for each entry; either way, you are increasing your odds.

If this all sounds too rich for your blood, trust me, that's what I thought at first, too. Let's put this all into a little bit of perspective, though, with two major recommendations for obtaining success in DFS:

DFS Success Tip #1: Start in cash contents if you are new to DFS. These will build your confidence as you learn to navigate lineups strategically and perform successfully. They'll also help build up your 'bank roll' slowly as well. When you play a friend in a standard redraft league every week, don't you have a 50% chance of winning? That's the thought process here too.

DFS Success Tip #2: Even as you gain more traction and want to start taking larger risks in GPP's/tournaments, you should keep a large percentage of your weekly games to cash ones (a lot of platforms recommend as high as 80%), as your odds are still relatively low in walking away with any money in the large, riskier contests. Continue considering tournament contests like a lottery ticket; you wouldn't quit your job to rely on lottery ticket buying/winnings solely. Keep playing the cash games to keep up your regular cash flow, and sprinkle in a few tournaments as well.

Side Note: There are an array of other DFS games to choose from as well. They don't fit directly in either of these popular categories precisely, but they tend to have similar qualities in their winning structure. Try out a few of them to see what piques your interest.

Best Ball Leagues

One of the most frustrating things about fantasy football is choosing the wrong starters to play every week. Adding free agents off waivers who don't perform well is a bummer, but isn't it worse when your bench players outperform the players you decided to start that week? Well, fret no more, as **best-ball** leagues will take away that stress.

These leagues are essentially standard leagues but without waivers, starters, or bench players – you just draft and see how many points the different players at each position score. If you have four running backs on your roster, for instance, and your league requires two in their standard 'starting lineup' (although you won't need to designate which two those are), whichever two running backs perform the best will have their point values added to your total for the week. This type of league brings a whole new level of importance to drafting as it is the *only* thing you will do the entire year.

Best ball leagues are typically Points Only (Total Points Scored) leagues so that your 'ultimate' roster's points each week are added up, and at the end of the regular season, the winner is the one who has the most points. As mentioned, while you can't (and there is no need) switch players around *within* your own roster, you also can't replace any either since there are no waivers. Hopefully, even after some injuries and bye weeks throughout the season, the depth of your roster is of high enough quality to carry your team to numerous points. If not, there's always next season? While this is a depressing thought, it's a pretty common one that you're bound to come across if you play long enough in any type of fantasy football league.

Tip 93: When competing in a best ball league, having an initial wager makes this a much more invigorating competition.

Entry fees for this variation of fantasy football – like DFS games – are standard on the offered platforms. Initial buy-ins that go towards an end-of-season payout in best-ball leagues tend to make it more worth the long-term investment since you don't get to change anything about your team throughout the season. It is an ultimate 'set it and forget it' fantasy football league, where your initial draft literally means *everything*. At least you can't make weekly mistakes, right? Speaking of: you'll probably come across some annoying friends in your standard, redraft leagues who are always pumped for the draft but become consistently inconsistent with adjusting their lineup each week. A best ball league may just be the perfect fit for them.

NFL Playoff Challenge

Tip 94: If you're craving more fantasy football after the NFL regular season is over, gather a few friends and participate in the NFL Playoff Challenge.

Outside of DFS, the rest of your fantasy league seasons are most likely coming to a close when the calendar strikes January. Some people may see this as a season well done and are happy to sit back and watch the real-life playoffs unfold. Others are itching for more options for multi-week fantasy competitions. As of the writing of this book, only NFL.com has this continued type of fantasy play for the NFL postseason, known as the **NFL Playoff Challenge**.

I. Rules and Strategies

Just like in most of the other leagues we've discussed, the positions are generally standard to select from one QB, two RBs, two WRs, one TE, a kicker, and a team defense/special teams unit (no bench players). Points are scored in a similar format to standard leagues as well. However, there are a few major rule tweaks that set this type of league aside from others:

Rule #1: Only players from the teams that advanced to the real-life NFL playoffs will be available to choose from in this accelerated four-week league. The four weeks of this mini-fantasy season align with the four rounds of the postseason: wild card round, divisional round, championship round, and the Super Bowl.

Rule #2: You are playing against your whole league in a Points Only (or Total Points Scored) format. At the end of the four weeks, whichever participant's team earned the most points hoist their own Lombardi Trophy.

Rule #3: Players on your roster for multiple weeks have a multiplier added to their points each consecutive week.

If the quarterback you selected for the wild card round wins their playoff game, they advance to the divisional round. Well, guess what? They also advance on your team. And to top it off, they are now awarded *double* the points they score in the divisional game, essentially rewarding you for picking a player from a winning squad. If they go on to win again, they will be earning you triple the points, and if they make it all the way to the Super Bowl, you guessed it: quadruple those points.

The downside to this is if you select a player who loses a game, you will have to start from scratch at that particular position the following week by finding a replacement for this player. That new player will begin with solely the number of points they score (no multipliers) since that would be their first week on your team. However, if this new player continues to advance in future rounds, they continue to increase their multiplier (depending on how many weeks they play on your roster).

Tip 95: Decide if you want to implement the 'bye week' technique when selecting players in the playoff challenge, as this can set you up for success or failure depending on the outcomes.

There are a few strategies that come into play when choosing players in this playoff challenge. Of course, it would be great to get some of the top-scoring players. Yet, if they are on a team that isn't expected to advance too far, it may be tough to start over at a position just a few rounds into the playoffs.

<u>Rule #4:</u> You can start a player with a bye week in the wild card round in your lineup.

This rule has the potential to fast-track your lineup. Specific teams in the NFL earn a first-round bye week in the playoffs, allowing them to proceed to the divisional round automatically without having to take part in the wild card round. If you choose a player from one of those teams to be in your lineup, unfortunately, they won't score you any points in that first week since they aren't participating. *But* if you decide to take that hit and start that player in the wild card round knowing he will get you a big goose egg, he will *automatically* score you double points in the divisional round (since you know that his team is advancing). A game where any player could be unavailable after any given game puts a riveting twist on reliability.

Tip 96: Try a few different strategies at different positions. If you feel you are struggling to catch up to your opponents, select a player you think will be scarcely owned.

Have fun with implementing various strategies into your decision making. I've had friends choose all of their players from one team before; I've seen it totally pay off (as that team advanced to the Super Bowl, giving *everyone* quadruple points). I have also seen it backfire with that team losing in the wild card round and having *zero* players with double points in the second round.

Side Note: One unique characteristic about this platform is that it *doesn't* allow you to see who the players on your opponents' lineups are each week. You can go back and look at a previous week to see who they had in their lineup to get a feel for who will have a multiplier, but you won't be able to see the replacements for any of the players that are officially out of the postseason. Not until after the games have started for that week.

If all else fails, aim for a player that you figure isn't 'owned' by many of your opponents. On the NFL.com platform, each player has a 'percentage owned' quantity next to their name. While this feature is available in most other fantasy league types (mostly just to show you trends in players), it can be beneficial because it shows you the odds you are up against if you want to 'go big or go home.' If you are down by a large number of points in the Super Bowl week and need a new running back, maybe your closest opponents have the starting running backs from both teams on multipliers. Why not get another running back from one of those teams? You won't be able to outscore them with the same player if you are just picking them up now (since they won't be on a multiplier for you), so glance at the percentages, take a chance, and shoot for the stars. It's the championship, after all!

Chapter 5 Review

In this chapter, you will learn about the following topics:

- Various specialized rules used to customize standard-league play
- Specific alterations and requirements to be successful in ongoing, dynasty league formats
- Standard types and unique strategies to enjoy the variety of Daily Fantasy Sports (DFS) available
- Basic rules to participate in best ball fantasy leagues
- Techniques to extend and enjoy your fantasy football season with the NFL Playoff Challenge

Conclusion: Final Words for an Exciting Journey Through the World of Fantasy Football

Well, you've made it! You blasted through the topics poured onto the pages of this book and can now officially start your exciting journey of managing your own personal fantasy football team. The rules, tips, and strategies provided throughout the past five chapters can be your guide through all of the ups and downs of a wild fantasy season.

For those of you who feel like this entire book would be better wrapped up into a nicely summed-up 'Plan of Action,' here's a brief overview of what you should take away and proceed with going forward:

- Know how your league settings operate because they are vital to playing the game successfully.

- Do *any* amount of research; it's better than none. A glance at some ADPs, do a mock draft or two or even turn on SportsCenter for an hour. Anything that can help you not bomb the draft is a significant first step in the right direction.

- Search for *value* and *volume*. These two terms describing a prospect can help you solve any conundrum that creeps up while you're on the clock during your draft. If a player is valuable to the balance of your team and you aren't reaching for them in your current round, grab him. If in doubt, someone who has a chance to touch the ball more than others can provide exceptional upside to your fantasy squad as well.

- Live and breathe for the waiver wire. Search this glorious platform for up-and-coming talent like a dog searches for that fallen potato chip under your side of the couch. Never be satisfied with your current roster. Do you know that season where I only had three players left from my originally-drafted team by the end of the year that I keep referring to? It actually didn't pan out as poorly as I have been leading on; I finished third in a 12-team league. Some of the most memorable waiver transactions I ever made happened that season; be relentless with pickups each week.

- Be curious. Try new things in fantasy football every year, week, or even every day. Make a season-changing trade, draft a late-round rookie, tell your commissioner you want to add a Superflex to your league next season, even throw ten bucks towards a Monday night cash DFS game. Exploring different avenues of adventure in fantasy football is what captures the attention of such a vast and unique audience.

Aside from that, I want to leave you with some closing thoughts on how to make the experience of leading a fantasy football team an unforgettable one:

Tip 97: Use your newfound knowledge of the rules, point systems, and position settings to improve the competition in your league.

Back in Chapter 1, we discussed the basics of how fantasy football leagues operate. After running through how to draft and manage your team in-season, we dove into specialized features to make your league even more competitive, depending on your league members' interests. Go forth with this information and help your league grow every year. Start suggesting interesting tweaks to different rules as you see them affecting teams throughout the season. Discuss the possibility of adding a position or changing the way one accumulates points if you feel it can give an extra edge to the game as you become more accustomed to it. Any thoughts you bring up to your league can potentially enhance *everyone's* experience, so don't be shy with your ideas.

Tip 98: Treat your draft like it's New Year's Day.

Every fantasy football manager feels refreshed right before a fantasy draft each season: a clean slate, new goals, and new people to help you get there. Sound familiar? Drafting your team may be a small part of your season in the grand scheme of things, but it is also the *start* to it. Treat your new fantasy year like many people do when the holidays wrap up in the winter; a brand-new year, a fresh new you (or, in this case, a fresh new fantasy team). And like I mentioned in the introduction to Chapter 2: treat this day as a grand event. Dare I say, like a New Year's Eve party?

Tip 99: Don't forget to cherish the good waiver moves just as much as you sulk over the bad ones.

I know I said you can't take the moves you make on the waiver wire too seriously. You may be flaunting something that you luckily stumbled on, only to be disappointed later. Or you may ruin your sound decision-making process because of an unlucky break that you later realize wasn't your fault at all. But you'll *live* on the waiver wire, so make it worthwhile. Definitely get excited (and make sure your fellow league members know it!) when your new waiver claim performs well. Also, be prepared to take lots of flack for giving up on what turned out to be a breakout performer that your opponent reaped the benefits from when they scooped him up. And of course, make sure to give your league challengers a hard time too, if they make a poor free agent move. Your moods will jump around with the adds and drops you make throughout the season, but your spirit should keep your love for the game intact.

Tip 100: Be a part of multiple leagues or league types to maximize your enjoyment of the sport.

From what you've learned about the wild array of league types in fantasy football, I highly suggest giving a few others a try. Don't rush into another league at first; managing one standard team will be a great start. Just don't shy away from others before giving them a shot. I have some friends who are strictly DFS players and don't play any other type of fantasy football; others live and breathe dynasty and think nothing else is captivating enough. Even if you just want to stick with standard leagues, maybe join two separate ones the following season to see how they differ (and to have two different teams of players to root for). Whatever you dive into as you advance in your journey with your new favorite hobby, there will always be new ways to keep the adventure exciting. If you stick with one standard league and that's good enough for you, that's fine too; it's all about optimizing your fun and love for the game.

You are officially geared with the proper tools to help you make wise yet valiant decisions as a fantasy manager. I will leave you with one last tip that will sum up your entire fantasy experience and, hopefully, everything you have taken away from this book:

Tip 101: The most successful fantasy football experiences are the most enjoyable ones, so relish every moment.

From all that you've soaked up over the last 35,000 or so words, you have plenty of methods to help you succeed at this amazing online game. Yet, true success is measured in the pure gratification you get from the sport. Winning always helps that, of course. But enjoying the sense of community that can be built and the passion for an aspect of the great sport of football that many don't realize exists will ensure you reap the ultimate benefits in your new world of fantasy football. Best of luck out there, and don't forget: draft running backs early and place those waiver claims!

About the Expert

Bobby Duke has been an avid NFL fan for over 25 years (*Go Pack Go!*) and has been playing, commissioning, and analyzing different strategies relating to fantasy football for close to two decades. He is currently a contributing writer for various popular sports websites, where he analyzes weekly fantasy football topics and trends. He also teaches discussion-based, football-centric classes for K-12 students via Outschool.com, an online education marketplace.

Bobby's love for the game of football stems from his lively interactions growing up watching the sport with family and friends. Since then, this interest has flourished into deep dive fantasy analysis, various league types, and watch-events every Sunday afternoon. Having been a science educator, education consultant, and sports coach for nearly a decade, Bobby has always had a true passion for creating genuine connections by helping people explore their interests. Using the strategic methods and active participation traits the game of fantasy football offers, he enjoys finding ways to help participants expand their knowledge – and love – for the sport.

You can stay connected to all things fantasy football with Bobby by following his Twitter handle: @TheBobbyDuke.

HowExpert publishes quick 'how to' guides on all topics from A to Z by everyday experts. Visit HowExpert.com to learn more.

Recommended Resources

- HowExpert.com – Quick 'How To' Guides on All Topics from A to Z by Everyday Experts.
- HowExpert.com/free – Free HowExpert Email Newsletter.
- HowExpert.com/books – HowExpert Books
- HowExpert.com/courses – HowExpert Courses
- HowExpert.com/clothing – HowExpert Clothing
- HowExpert.com/membership – HowExpert Membership Site
- HowExpert.com/affiliates – HowExpert Affiliate Program
- HowExpert.com/jobs – HowExpert Jobs
- HowExpert.com/writers – Write About Your #1 Passion/Knowledge/Expertise & Become a HowExpert Author.
- HowExpert.com/resources – Additional HowExpert Recommended Resources
- YouTube.com/HowExpert – Subscribe to HowExpert YouTube.
- Instagram.com/HowExpert – Follow HowExpert on Instagram.
- Facebook.com/HowExpert – Follow HowExpert on Facebook.

Milton Keynes UK
Ingram Content Group UK Ltd.
UKHW011947110823
426759UK00002B/12

9 781648 917110